The 101 Most Important UNIX and Linux Commands

Ronald J. Leach

1st Edition

Leach, Ronald J.

The 101 Most Important UNIX And Linux Commands/Ronald J. Leach

p. 148 cm.

Includes bibliographical references

ISBN: 9781939142061 (digital version)

ISBN-13: 978-1939142306 (print version)

ISBN-10: 193914230X (print version)

1. Operating Systems (Computers 2. UNIX (Computer file)

I. Title: The 101 Most Important UNIX and Linux Commands

Books by Ronald J. Leach

Software and Computer Industry

Using C in Software Design

Using C in Software Design, Second Edition *

Advanced Topics in UNIX

Advanced Topics in UNIX, Second Edition *

The 101 Most Important UNIX and Linux Commands *

Software Reuse: Methods, Models, Costs

Software Reuse: Methods, Models, Costs, Second Edition *

Fastest Paths to a Job in the Computer Industry *

Object-Oriented Design and Programming in C++

Introduction to Software Engineering

Data Recovery *

Computer Forensics Workbook (available 2013) *

Identity Theft

Identity Theft in the Cyber Age

Identity Theft in the Cyber Age *

Twelve and a Half Steps to Avoid Identity Theft *

Genealogy

Relative Genealogy

Genealogy for the Information Age (Originally printed as Computers and Logic in Genealogy)

Fiction

Why 2K? *

Eat Kids At School *

The Baltimore Authors Series

Six by Mencken and one by Nietzsche *

Many by Key and one by Weybright *

Many by Poe, Dickinson, Nash, Key, and Other Baltimore Poets *

Many by Douglass and DuBois *

Seven by Sinclair *

Tubman, Douglass, and Other Maryland Slave Narratives*

Etiquette in Society, in Business, in Politics, and at Home + The Title Market *

Four Novels and a Travelogue of Emily Post *

More by Mencken *

Mencken and Nietzsche *

The Early Dos Passos Reader *

A Christopher Morley Reader *

A Fitzgerald Reader *

A Gertrude Stein Reader *

A Frederick Douglass Reader *

A W. E. B. DuBois Reader *

The Crevice *

Baltimore Hats *

Baltimore its History and its People-Vol. I *

Baltimore its History and its People-Vol. II *

Baltimore its History and its People-Vol. III *

Voyages to America *
A Colonial America Reader *
A Carter G. Woodson Reader *
Black and Native American Soldiers in the Civil War *
Troy, the Iliad, The Odyssey, and More *
Two Dictionaries: Old and Middle English *

Classic Martian Stories, Vol. 1 *
Classic Martian Stories, Vol. 2 *
Classic Martian Stories, Vol. 3 *
Classic Martian Stories, Vol. 4 *
Classic Martian Stories, Vol. 5 *
Classic Martian Stories, Vol. 6 *
Classic Martian Stories, Vol. 7 *
Tales of Atlantis *

*** Ebook Edition**

Table of Contents

1. Introduction

Learning UNIX, including the most common variants (Linux, Apple Darwin, Mach, Solaris, BSD, FreeBSD, HP-UX, Xenix, AIX, AUX, etc.) is often a daunting task for both novice and relatively experienced users. The problem is the complexity of UNIX itself. To complicate matters, there are multiple Linux versions: Red Hat (now Fedora), Ubuntu, SUSE, and Debian are the most common. Linux itself was created by Linus Torvalds who, while a student at the University of Helsinki, was motivated to create a new kernel that would have the same functionality as UNIX and MINIX. (MINIX was created by Professor Andrew Tanenbaum of the *Vrije Universiteit* in The Netherlands as a small modifiable version of UNIX that could be used for teaching purposes.) These UNIX versions have much more in common than they have differences, although the differences, when they occur, can be confusing even to an experienced user. As much as possible, we will focus on the commonality and discuss the major differences as appropriate.

Why is it so hard to understand UNIX? The UNIX operating system is entirely too large to be described in detail in any series of books, much less in a single book! Here's an illustration of this point. Mark G. Sobell has written an excellent series of books on UNIX and Linux. Some titles in the series are:

- *A Practical Guide to Linux Commands, Editors, and Shell Programming (3rd Edition)* – 1154 pages
- *A Practical Guide to Fedora and Red Hat Enterprise Linux, Sixth Edition* – 1266 pages

- *A Practical Guide to Ubuntu Linux (3rd Edition)* – 1251 pages

Clearly, there are sufficient differences between just these three variants to justify these large books devoted to a single variant. And these books only treat variants of Linux!

There are more than 2000 entries for common commands, system calls, and utilities in many on-line UNIX manuals. Unfortunately, using on-line manuals as the only source of information can be confusing and time-consuming. As an example, the associated on-line manual pages on one Solaris system implementation required 7234 megabytes for storage of the 2545 entries on disk. This is equivalent to more than 1400 pages of text! To make matters even more complicated, most system calls can have multiple arguments, many of which interact with other arguments, and the number and order in which these arguments occur can also vary. The combination of system calls with a typical number of arguments results in a syntax approximately as rich as the active vocabulary of the average high school graduate in the United States.

The spelling is also daunting to the new UNIX user. Why, for example, is there a system call named creat() instead of create()? Why is *umount* not spelled *unmount*? It makes no sense to anyone today, and may not have done so, even when these names were given. Of course, unusual spelling makes it even more difficult for anyone looking up these names in an on-line manual of commands.

Even after learning all this information in detail, you would be able to learn only the syntax and common error codes associated with these commands, system calls, and utilities. We'll simplify matters here by limiting ourselves to what I judge to be the most important system calls and shell commands and for these, we will limit our discussion to the most important function arguments. My judgment of what is important is based on several things:

- my experience as a professor teaching both novice and advanced students of UNIX over twenty times in classes on operating systems,
- my experience as an author of two books on UNIX,
- and my experience as a consultant who, while doing quality checks on software, analyzed many software systems running on UNIX and Linux operating systems and comprising hundreds of thousands of lines of code across several different application domains.

The system calls and shell commands that we will discuss here in this book are listed below. in alphabetical order. For clarity, we have indicated which ones are system calls by using parentheses. We have also grouped related commands on the same line.

Here is the alphabetical list:

accept()
awk
bind()
cat
cc
gcc
cd
chdir
chmod
chown
chroot
close()
connect()
cp
cpio
creat()
crontab
csplit, split
df
diff

du

dup

echo

edit, ed, sed, vi

exec

exec, execlp(), execle(), execvp(), execve()

exit()

file

find

finger

for, foreach, do, done, if, ... (built-in shell commands)

fork()

ftp

getopt, getopt()

getuid(), geteuid(), getgid(), getegid()

grep

head

man

IPC commands

ipcs

ipcstat

kill

listen()

ln

logout

lp

lpstat

ls

make

mkdir

mkfifo()

more

mount

msgctl()

msgget()

msgrcv()

msgsnd()

mv

newgrp

nice()

nmake

nslookup

open()

passwd

ping

pipe()

ps

pwd

rcmd

- rcp
- read()
- restore
- rlogin
- rm
- rmdir
- RPC commands
- rsh
- semctl()
- semget()
- semop()
- send()
- set
- setuid(), seteuid(), setgid(), setegid()
- sh, csh, ksh, bash, posix shells
- shmat()
- shmctl()
- shmdt()
- shmget()
- shutdown
- signal()
- sleep()
- socket()
- ssh
- system()
- tail
- tar, ar, bar, rar, gzip, gunzip, zcat
- telnet
- thread commands
- touch
- umask
- umount
- uname
- wait()
- wc
- who, whoami, whois
- write()

Here is how the rest of this book is organized. In the rest of this introductory chapter there are two additional sections. One will provide an overview of UNIX and the other will describe the basics of UNIX system architecture.

Chapter 2 discusses the 101 most important UNIX shell commands and system calls. We provide the syntax of each of them, followed by a discussion of their design, usage and pitfalls, followed by examples of their most common usage.

There are two appendices. Appendix 1 is entitled "The Most Essential UNIX Files." In this appendix, we discuss the important files stdout, stdin, and stderr. We will also discuss file descriptors; the redirection commands <, <<, >, and >>; and how to use simple shell commands to do things such as redirect the contents of the errors in stderr to an error log file. Appendix 1 also contains a description of i-nodes and i-numbers to help explain some of the system calls, as well as a discussion of the differences between i-nodes in UNIX and Linux systems.

Appendix 2 is entitled "The Most Essential C Functions" and includes a discussion of what I have found to be the most useful functions in the standard C library, plus a few useful functions from the math library. Functions such as memcpy(), which are not really system calls, are discussed here.

The book closes with a short list of relevant references.

1.1 Overview Of UNIX

UNIX is designed to be a powerful general purpose operating system that allows multiple users to use the computer at any one time and allows each of these users to be able to run many concurrent processes. It is currently implemented on a large variety of computers with different hardware architectures including: personal computers with a single processing core, personal computers with a multicore architecture, workstations, minicomputers, mainframes, supercomputers, and parallel computers. Many important software applications have versions that run on computers using some the UNIX operating system or some variant thereof.

The UNIX operating system was originally developed at AT&T Bell Laboratories by Dennis Ritchie and Ken Thompson. Their goal was to develop a small but powerful operating system that would be easily ported to computers other than the one for which the system was initially developed. UNIX had several important features.

- It had an elegant view of the features of an operating system in that every essential feature could be classified as either a file or a process.
- Files were streams of bytes, with any other structure of the file imposed by the application program accessing the file. No assumption about file organization such as database design, size of records, etc, was made by the operating system. Thus there was a high level of portability of applications programs because the high-level information about file organization was described in the application, not the operating system. The file system had a hierarchical, tree-like design.
- The software was written in layers with only the lowest level of software, called the kernel, being able to access the hardware directly.
- It was largely written in the C programming language, with about ten percent written in assembly language, instead of being entirely written in the assembly language of the host computer. (C was developed at the same time at AT&T Bell Laboratories.) Thus most of the code was portable from one platform to another. As mentioned above, Linus Torvalds wrote the Linux kernel in C.

- The command interpreter used for the user interface was a powerful programming language called the UNIX shell. It included facilities for the execution of processes, combination of processes into larger processes, as well as the control structures and variables that are typically found in programming languages. Multiple shells are now available: the Bourne shell, C shell, bash (Bourne again) shell, POSIX shell, and Korn shell are the most popular, with the bash shell being the default shell for Linux and Macintosh systems. (Generally speaking, the bash shell is a superset of the Bourne shell.) For simplicity of discussion, we will use the term "shell" without modification whenever we encounter a shell command that works in all common UNIX shells. A Wikipedia entry for "Comparison of Command Shells" provides a summary of differences between these and other UNIX command shells.
- The operating system allowed multiple users to run their processes by interleaving execution on the same CPU. The scheduling of processes was dynamic and was intended to maximize throughput. A process that was I/O intensive received ready access to the CPU when it needed it. A CPU-intensive process could not control all the CPU cycles but was given reasonable access to computing resources. (The concurrency allowed by having processes has been extended to lightweight processes and threads for efficiency reasons, especially in a heavily networked environment.)

1.2 UNIX System Architecture

UNIX was developed according to an extremely simple and elegant design principle that two types of objects comprise the entire system: files and processes. This simplicity of design and the resulting computing power have allowed UNIX to become a popular operating system. It has also been the prime motivation for UNIX users and application programmers to follow the discipline of designing new software while keeping with the original philosophy of a layered software architecture. A layered software architecture is one in which lower level details are hidden by combining them as needed into larger software units.

The layered software architecture of UNIX is described in Figure 1.1 below. The "syscall vector" provides the interface from the system call to the kernel and is not discussed further in this book. For more information on the syscall vector, see my book *Advanced Topics in UNIX*, the second edition of which is available on this ebook platform.

In this book we will concentrate on the most important UNIX system calls and the shell commands that often encompass them.

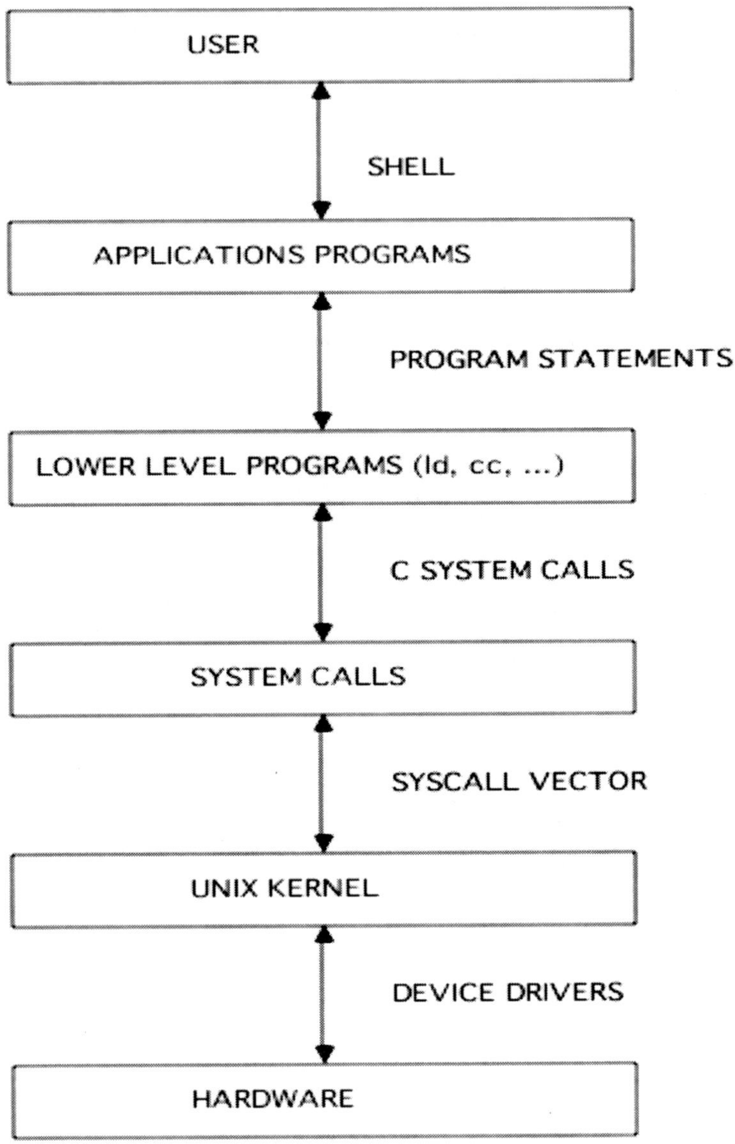

Figure 1.1 UNIX software architecture.

2. The Most Important UNIX and Linux System Calls and Shell Commands

The important system calls and shell commands that we discuss in this book were listed in alphabetical order in the introduction. Now we present them differently. For pedagogical reasons, these important system calls and commands are grouped into several different categories, depending on the most likely roles that a user of the system call or shell command will have in his or her use of the computer's operating system. For each of these system calls or shell commands, we give the formal syntax, a description of the purpose of the system call or shell command, and the most likely usage. In some cases where the concepts are complex, we will provide a longer discussion of the system call or shell command.

Commands an Ordinary User Will Find Especially Useful

1. ls

Syntax: ls [-ABCFGHLOPRSTUW@abcdefghiklmnopqrstuwx1] [file ...]

ls shell command – This shell command is used for listing files in a directory. It has many options. The formal syntax is overwhelming and most of the options are almost never needed. If no options are given, all files in the current directory are listed, except for those whose name begins with the dot, or period, character, '.' Since the optional file argument can be either a relative file name such as ../dir/file1, or an absolute one such as /usr/tmp/dir/file1, the contents of any directory that is readable by the user can be listed.

The most important options are: the 'a' character for listing all directory names beginning with the dot character, the 'l' character for listing the names as well as information about the size of each of the files in the directory, and the 'R' character for listing the contents of each directory file recursively. The 'i' option, which is used much less often, prints the names of the files in the directory together with their i-numbers. (We will discuss i-numbers in Appendix 1 when we discuss i-nodes.) Many of the other options are used for formatting the output of the ls utility shell command and are rarely used in practice.

USAGE:

ls

ls file1 file 2

ls -al

ls -alR

ls -i

2. rm

Syntax: rm [-dfiPRrvW] file ...

rm shell command – This shell command removes files from a directory. The most important option is 'R' or its equivalent 'r;' both remove all files in the current working directory. Note that this does not remove the file's data from the disk! In this age of rampant identity theft, the 'I' option can be useful, since it enables overwriting of the contents of the deleted file three times with three different patterns, thereby making life more difficult for any potential identity thieves.

USAGE:

rm -r file_name

WARNING: This command allows wildcards, so it is possible to accidentally delete many files. The example below shows this. It will remove **all** files in the current working directory, and then try to remove a single file named ".c" Notice the (intentional) space between the * and the .c at the end of the command.

rm -r * .c

You can avoid this potential disaster in three ways: by setting a "noclobber" option, by using the 'i' option to require you to respond 'y' before deleting, or by simply removing your hands from the keyboard and checking that you have not created a massive typo before you hit the return key.

3. find

Syntax: find [-H | -L | -P] [-EXdsx] [-f path] path ...[expression]

or

find [-H | -L | -P] [-EXdsx] -f path [path ...] [expression] find shell command – This command allows a user to search for a file within a directory. Unlike most shell commands described here in this book, the most important part of the syntax is in the optional path and optional expression at the end of the command. We illustrate this with the most common use of this command: to find a file and print its name and location.

USAGE:

find . -name file_name -print

Let's parse this command. We are looking at the path from the current working directory, which is denoted by a dot character. The command looks for a file whose name is "file_name" and then prints the name of the file. If there are more than one such file, then the name of each of these files is printed.

We could use any other legitimate path, specified as either an absolute path, as in

find / -name file_name -print

or a relative path, as in

find ../ -name file_name -print

Wild cards are also allowed; hence, we can list all files in a system using

find / -name * -print

4. cp

Syntax: cp [-R [-H | -L | -P]] [-fi | -n] [-apvX] source_file target_file

or

cp [-R [-H | -L | -P]] [-fi | -n] [-apvX] source_file ... Target_directory cp shell command – This command allows one file to be copied either to another file or to another directory. Recursion is allowed using the 'R' option.

USAGE:

cp file_1 file_2

or

cp file_1 new_directory

5. cat

Syntax: cat [-benstuv] [file ...]

cat shell command – The word "cat" is a shortened version of the word "concatenate," which refers to the addition of one file to another in sequence. The cat shell command sends the contents of a file to another file, which may be the terminal display file; that is, the computer's display screen. Some UNIX haters have been known to ask if, since the "cat" command shows a file on the screen, is there a "dog" command to print a file?

This command is often used with the > and >> characters to redirect output.

USAGE:

cat file_name

or

cat file_1 > file_2

or

cat file_1 file_2 >> combined_file

This last command copies the first file, file_1, to the file named combined_file and then appends the contents of the second file to combined_file. This, of course, justifies the use of the term "concatenation."

6. grep

Syntax: grep [options] PATTERN [FILE...]

or

grep [options] [-e PATTERN | -f FILE] [FILE...]

grep shell command – This command is used for matching patterns within a file. All lines within the files being searched that contain the desired pattern are printed. The pattern must be what is known as a "regular expression." For more information on what constitutes a regular expression, consult any book on compiler writing or comparative computer languages.

In our first usage example, we are searching for the seven-letter pattern "My_Name" in all files (hence the use of the wild card) within the current working directory. In the second usage example, we show that the pattern of letters is what matters in the regular expression used in the grep command, not a character string enclosed in quotes.

In the third example, we are looking for a positive integer of one or more digits within a file named "file_name." Note that in this example, the asterisk '*' is not used as a wild card. The syntax of the regular expression [1-9[0-9]* indicates that the first character to be searched for is a digit in the range 1 through 9, followed by 0 or more occurrences of the digits 0 through 9. (The left bracket '[' is <u>not</u> part of the regular expression.)

USAGE:

grep "My_Name" *

or

grep My_Name *

or

grep [1-9[0-9]* file_name

7. lp

Syntax: lp [-E] [-U username] [-c] [-d destination[/instance]] [-h hostname[:port]] [-m] [-n num_copies] [-o option[=value]] [-q priority] [-s] [-t title] [-H handling] [-P page-list] [--] [file(s)]

or

lp [-E] [-U username] [-c] [-h hostname[:port]] [-i job-id] [-n num-copies] [-o option[=value]] [-q priority] [-t title] [-H handling] [-P page-list]

lp shell command – This is the classical UNIX command to print a file. The name of the command comes from the old term "line printer." Most users will use the form below.

USAGE:

lp file_name

8. more, less

Syntax: less -?

or

less --help

or

less -V

or

less --version

or

less [-[+]aBcCdeEfFgGiIJKLmMnNqQrRsSuUVwWX~]
[-b space] [-h lines] [-j line] [-k keyfile]
[-{oO} logfile] [-p pattern] [-P prompt] [-t tag]
[-T tagsfile] [-x tab,...] [-y lines] [-[z] lines]
[-# shift] [+[+]cmd] [--] [filename]...

more, less shell commands – The more shell command, and its successor, the less shell command, are used to page through a file line by line. There are two primary differences between these two commands: the *more* command pages forward through a file, whereas the *less* command can go both backward and forward; and the less command starts working without waiting for the entire file to be loaded into memory. Most of the options are rarely used, since the formatting they provide often takes more time than simply paging through the file.

NOTE: The two commands work on both text tiles and binary files, although using their use on binary files rarely has a useful purpose.

USAGE:

more file_name

less file_name

9. chown

Syntax: chown [-fhv] [-R [-H | -L | -P]] owner[:group] file ...

or

chown [-fhv] [-R [-H | -L | -P]] :group file ...

chown shell command – This command changes the ownership of a file. Technically, this changes the user ID of a file. There is an option to change the group of an owner also, using a command chgrp. Technically, this changes the group ID.

USAGE:

chown some_other_user file_name

10. chmod

Syntax: chmod [-fv] [-R [-H | -L | -P]] mode file ...

or

chmod [-fv] [-R [-H | -L | -P]] [-a | +a | =a] ACE file ...

or

chmod [-fhv] [-R [-H | -L | -P]] [-E] file ...

or

chmod [-fhv] [-R [-H | -L | -P]] [-C] file ...

or

chmod [-fhv] [-R [-H | -L | -P]] [-N] file ...

chmod shell command – This command allows the mode of a file to be changed. Generally speaking, the mode of a file is an octal number that reflects the file's access permissions. Historically, the permissions were written as three octal digits, chosen from 'r,' 'w,' and 'x,' reflecting three types of permissions: read, write and execute (search, in the case of a directory). Some newer systems have a fourth octal bit.

Possible permissions and their octal encodings are given below:

0001 For files, this permission allows execution by anyone, including the owner. For directories, this allows others to search in the directory.

0002 Allow writing by others.

0004 Allow reading by others.

0010 For files, this allows execution by group members. For directories, this allows all group members to search in the directory.

0020 Allow writing by group members.

0040 Allow reading by group members.

0100 For files, allow execution by the owner. For directories, allow the owner to search in the directory.

0200 Allow writing by owner.

0400 Allow reading by owner.

Additional octal bits, which should not be used by the inexperienced user, are:

4000 (the set-user-ID-on-execution bit) Executable files with this bit set will run with effective uid set to the uid of the file owner. Directories with the set-user-id bit set will force all files and sub-directories created in them to be owned by the directory owner and not by the uid of the creating process, if the underlying file system supports this feature.

For more information, see the man pages chmod(2) and the suiddir option to mount(8). These man pages can be found by typing

man 2 chmod

or

man 8 suiddir

2000 (the set-group-ID-on-execution bit) Executable files with this bit set will run with effective gid set to the gid of the file owner.

1000 (the sticky bit) See chmod(2) and sticky(8). To examine these particular manual entries, type

man 2 chmod

or

man 8 sticky.

USAGE:

chmod +777 file (removes all restrictions on file access)

chmod +x file (makes file "executable")

11. set

Syntax: set

or

set var_name=value

set shell command – This shell command is used for two purposes: to list the values of all shell variables using the simple syntax of just the word "set," and to assign values to existing or new shell variables.

USAGE:

set

or

set var=value

12. mkdir

Syntax: mkdir [-pv] [-m mode] directory_name ...

mkdir shell command – This command makes a directory within the current working directory. While there are options to change the mode of a newly created directory using this command, it is probably easier to create a directory with the desired mode in two steps: making the directory with mkdir and then changing its mode with chmod, rather than worrying about how to use the hard-to-remember syntax of the mkdir command.

USAGE:

mkdir directory_name

13. rmdir

Syntax: rmdir [-p] directory ...

rmdir shell command – This command removes directories. Note that multiple directories can be removed by this command. Use of the -p argument means that each directory argument is treated as a pathname of which all components will be removed, if they are empty, starting with the last most component. It is probably best for novice UNIX users to avoid the use of this argument.

USAGE:

rmdir directory_name

14. cd

Syntax: cd directory_name

cd shell command – This shell command changes the current working directory to the one specified in the argument, which identifies the target directory. The target directory can be specified using either an absolute or a relative path name.

USAGE:

cd directory_name

15. chdir()

Syntax:

int chdir(const char *path);

chdir() system call – Like the cd shell command, this system call allows the user to change the current working directory. However, as a system call, chdir() is used within programs rather than just as a stand-alone command within a UNIX or Linux shell.

USAGE:

chdir (new_dir_name);

16. mv

Syntax: mv [-f | -i | -n] [-v] source target

or

mv [-f | -i | -n] [-v] source ... directory

mv shell command – This shell command moves files. In the case of a single source and a single target, one file is moved to the other; that is, renamed. If the final argument is a directory, files are moved to it. If the -i option is selected, the user is prompted before a move occurs.

USAGE:

mv file_1 file_2

or

mv file_1 file_2 file_3 new_dir

17. pwd

Syntax:

pwd shell command – This shell command prints the current working directory, whose value is stored in the shell variable cwd. The pwd command has no arguments.

USAGE:

pwd

18. df

Syntax: df [-b | -h | -H | -k | -m | -g | -P] [-ailn] [-t] [-T type] [file | filesystem ...]

df shell command – The df shell command indicates the total amount of free disk space used by filesystems. It is commonly used with no argument. If a filesystem is selected as an argument, then information is provided only for that filesystem. As an example, running the df command on my MacBook Air shows the following information for the file system mounted on the location /dev/disk0s2. (Some data has been omitted.) From my perspective, the most important data is that the disk is only 30% full.

```
Filesystem     512-blocks     Used Available Capacity  Mounted on
/dev/disk0s2    235298960 69774368 165012592    30%    /
```

USAGE: df

df file_system

19. du

Syntax: du [-H | -L | -P] [-a | -s | -d depth] [-c] [-h | -k | -m | -g] [-x] [-I mask] [file ...]

du shell command – The du shell command provides information that complements what is produced by the df shell command. It provides information on files, but primarily on a directory by directory basis. If no argument is supplied, which is the most common usage, then du examines the current working directory and produces the size on the disk of each file and each directory within the current working directory.

USAGE:

du

20. awk

Syntax: awk [-F fs] [-v var=value] ['prog' | -f progfile] [file ...]

awk shell command – This shell command actually invokes the awk programming language which was invented by A. V. Aho, B. W. Kernighan, and P. J. Weinberger. The language was developed to match patterns within files.

I found this programming language especially useful in 1993, when I was a Faculty Fellow at NASA and was writing programs to evaluate the complexity of some existing C and UNIX programs. I had broken a bone near my right elbow and had a very large, awkward cast, so typing was extremely difficult, and multiple character presses using the shift and other keys were excruciatingly painful. I could get the job done using awk, which, among all programming languages that I studied, required the least amount of typing, including the least amount of multiple key presses. (I broke three keyboards during the two months my arm was in the cast.)

USAGE:

awk -f awk_program_file input_file

21. finger

Syntax: finger [-46gklmpsho] [user ...] [user@host ...]

finger shell command – The finger shell command provides information about users on a system. On my system, the finger command, with no arguments, produced information in the following fields on each user:

Login Name TTY Idle Login Time Office Phone

USAGE:

finger

22. ssh

Syntax: ssh [-1246AaCfgKkMNnqsTtVvXxYy] [-b bind_address] [-c cipher_spec] [-D [bind_address:]port] [-e escape_char]

[-F configfile] [-I pkcs11] [-i identity_file] [-L [bind_address:]port:host:hostport] [-l login_name]

[-m mac_spec] [-O ctl_cmd] [-o option] [-p port] [-R [bind_address:]port:host:hostport] [-S ctl_path]

[-W host:port] [-w local_tun[:remote_tun]] [user@]hostname [command]

ssh shell command – The ssh shell command is a program for logging into a remote machine and for executing commands on that remote machine. It is intended to eventually replace rlogin and rsh, and provide secure encrypted communications between two untrusted hosts over an insecure network. Do not use this shell command unless you are highly conversant with both UNIX shells and networking.

USAGE:

See the ssh man page

23. rsh

Syntax: rsh [-46dn] [-l username] [-t timeout] host [command]

rsh shell command – The rsh shell command runs a remote shell on another UNIX host. For security purposes, ssh is preferred to rsh.

USAGE:

rsh host_name command

Commands a Shell Programmer Will Find Especially Useful

24. ed, sed, vi, vim

Syntax: ed [-] [-sx] [-p string] [file]

or

sed [-Ealn] command [file ...]

or

sed [-Ealn] [-e command] [-f command_file] [-i extension] [file ...]

or

vim [options] [file ..]

or

vim [options] -

or

vim [options] -t tag

or

vim [options] -q [errorfile]

or

ex

or

view

or

gvim gview evim eview

or

rvim rview rgvim rgview

Editing shell commands – These shell commands are useful for editing simple files – either text files or source code files – without having to obtain the knowledge, and managing the overhead, of an integrated development environment (IDE).

USAGE:

vim file_name

vi file_name

25. for, foreach, do, done, if, ...

Syntax: multiple commands can be used within UNIX shells such as the Bourne shell, C shell, bash shell, Korn shell, and POSIX shell. These built-in commands are:

builtin, !, %, ., :, @, {, }, alias, alloc, bg, bind, bindkey, break, breaksw, builtins, case, cd, chdir, command, complete, continue, default, dirs, do, done, echo, echotc, elif, else, end, endif, endsw, esac, eval, exec, exit, export, false, fc, fg, filetest, fi, for, foreach, getopts, glob, goto, hash, hashstat, history, hup, if, jobid, jobs, kill, limit, local, log, login, logout, ls-F, nice, nohup, notify, onintr, popd, printenv, pushd, pwd, read, readonly, rehash, repeat, return, sched, set, setenv, settc, setty, setvar, shift, source, stop, suspend, switch, telltc, test, then, time, times, trap, true, type, ulimit, umask, unalias, uncomplete, unhash, unlimit, unset, unsetenv, until, wait, where, which, while

Here is an example of a simple shell program, known as a "shell script," to perform a particular action that could be used for program testing. It shows several features: comments, a for-loop to control iteration, redirection of input and output, a call to the diff shell command, the use of a pipe to connect the output of one process to the input of another process, and a call to the wc shell command. This limited example illustrates the power of the built-in features of UNIX shells.

```
# Bourne shell script to compare the output of
# two programs named program1 and program2
# on five test files.
for i in test*
        do
                program1 < $i >> out1
                program2 < $i >> out2
        Done
# Now compare the output files.
# If they are identical we will produce 0.
```

diff out1 out2 | wc - l

Contrast this Bourne shell program to a C shell program to do the same thing where the for-loop syntax would be something like the following. Note the different reserved words and delimiters.

```
foreach i (file*.c)
        program1 < $i >> out1
        program2 < $i >> out2
end
```

The Bourne, bash, C, Korn, and POSIX shells are discussed briefly in item 42. You should also consult the man pages for more information.

Various shell commands – used for shell operation and programming.

USAGE:

Usage varies

26. crontab, at

Syntax: crontab [-u user] file

or

crontab [-u user] { -l | -r | -e }

or

at [-q x] [-f file] [-m] time

or

at -c job [job ...]

or

at [-f file] -t [[CC]YY]MMDDhhmm[.SS]

or

at -r job [job ...]

or

at -l -q queuename

or

at -l [job ...]

crontab shell command – The crontab shell command is used to schedule processes to execute at certain times. It is related to the cron shell command, which acts to make sure that the processes scheduled in crontab are actually executing. The crontab file is not intended to be directly changed by a user except by using an editor.

at shell command – The at command can be used to begin a job at a particular time. Typical uses for this are system backups to tape, or long compilations, which may take place late at night. The syntax of this shell command is

at options time date week script

and is interpreted by the shell to execute the set of shell commands called script at the specified time. The options include -c for executing script from the C shell and -s for executing the script from the Bourne shell; if no option is specified, then the shell that was set in the variable SHELL will be used for execution control. An example of this might be

at 3am week make project

which uses the UNIX make facility to create a (presumably very large) software system called project.

NOTES: The syntax of the crontab shell command is not standard across UNIX implementations.

The cron command is supplanted to a degree in Apple Darwin by the launchd command. (As a general rule, a UNIX or Linux command whose name ends in a 'd' is a "daemon" that wakes up and performs some operation.)

USAGE:

crontab -l (displays current crontab information for the current user)

crontab -e editor_name (allows the crontab file to be edited)

27. echo

Syntax: echo [-n] [string ...]

echo shell command – This shell command is used to send a message to the display screen. It is often used to provide a user information on the progress of a multi-step shell program to perform some action rather than leave the user wondering if the program is still running.

USAGE:

echo "MESSAGE"

28. diff

Syntax: diff [OPTIONS]... FILES

diff shell command – This shell command is used to illustrate the differences between two files. In the most common uses, it is applied to text files, source code files, or, more generally, to any files created with printable characters. The output generally consists of lines beginning with either a '<' or a '>' character, reflecting the fact that a line of "text" is in either the first file, but not the second file, or the opposite, respectively.

When applied to non-text files, the diff command usually produces output something like:

Binary files file_1 and file_2 differ.

You can compare two binary (non-text) files by using the -a option, although the output may be difficult to read.

USAGE:

diff file_1 file_2

29. file

Syntax: file [-bcdDhiIkLnNprsvz] [--mime-type] [--mime-encoding] [-f namefile] [-m magicfiles] [-M magicfiles] file

or

file -C [-m magicfiles]

or

file [--help]

file shell command – The file shell command attempts to determine the nature of the contents of a file by examining the first few bytes. The file command takes both text files and binary files as input. Text files are often characterized as being C source code files, C++ source code files, FORTRAN source code files, Java source code files, header files, and the like. Directory files are almost always characterized as directories by the file command.

Binary files, such as executable files, are often identified by examining a special byte called the Magic Number that indicates the presence of a file in the a.out, coff (Common Object FIle Format), or elf (Extensible Linking Format) format that is specific to object files that can be linked into executable files, or executable files, themselves.

Unfortunately, some of the results of the find command are incorrect for binary files. For example, on my MacBook Air running Darwin, a file created with the Apple Pages word processing software was incorrectly classified as a Zip archive data, requiring at least v2.0 in order to extract information. However, a file created with Microsoft Word was identified correctly, and some metadata was printed, including the author, date of creation, size, and so on. Source cde files for several different C and C++ programs were identified correctly.

USAGE:

file file_name

file *

30. ln

Syntax: ln [-Ffhinsv] source_file [target_file]

or

ln [-Ffhinsv] source_file ... target_dir

or

link source_file target_file

ln shell command – The ln shell command links one file to another. See the unlink() command for more information.

USAGE:

ln file_1 file_2

31. cc, gcc, c++, g++

Syntax: gcc [-c|-S|-E] [-std=standard]

[-g] [-pg] [-Olevel]

[-Wwarn...] [-pedantic]

[-Idir...] [-Ldir...]

[-Dmacro[=defn]...] [-Umacro]

[-foption...] [-mmachine-option...]

[-o outfile] [@file] infile...

compiler shell commands – These shell commands invoke the various compilers. Generally, a compiler on a UNIX or Linux system whose name begins with 'g' is a product of the Free Software Foundation's gnu project; those whose name begins with 'c' are probably produced by, or licensed by, the hardware vendor.

The most important options of most compilers are:

- the -O option that provides an attempt to improve the performance of the executable file by turning on an optimizing program within the compiler
- the -o option, which forces creation of an *object* file (for combination with other object files to make an executable file)
- the -p option, which turns on profiling, so that a software engineer interested in improving run-time performance can see which parts of the executable code take the longest to execute.

Most of the options are of use only to highly experienced users and there are some options that are available only on certain systems.

USAGE:

cc file.c

cc -o file1.c

cc -O file1.c

cc -p file1.c

32. make, nmake

Syntax: make [-f makefile] [options] ... [targets] ...

make shell command – The make utility allows programmers to create projects that are too large to be coded within a single source code file but may require tens, hundreds, and even thousands of source code files. Many software systems are so large and complex that they are developed by geographically separated software teams. Through the use of files often known as makefiles or Makefiles, the make utility, and the related nmake utility, these complex systems can be managed. Proper management allows a change in one source file to be reflected in other source code files making up the same program.

The make utility greatly speeds up the creation of executable files created from multiple source code files. When make is invoked after one or more of the source code files is changed, only the files that have been changed since the last application of the make command are recompiled and linked into an executable file, rather than recompiling everything. This is an enormous time saving.

Large software systems that require makefiles are often created under some system for keeping track of changes in programs, a process known as configuration management. A utility known as sccs (Source Code Control System) is often helpful in configuration management.

Note that many complex modern software systems are developed within integrated development environments (IDEs) that incorporate the capabilities of make, nmake, and sccs. However, many applications, especially those made available from the Free Software Foundation and sourceforge.net, require the use of the make or nmake utilities in order to install them after downloads of source code files.

USAGE:

make -f makefile

33. csplit, split

Syntax: csplit [-ks] [-f prefix] [-n number] file args ...

or

split [-a suffix_length] [-b byte_count[k|m]] [-l line_count] [-p pattern] [file [name]]

csplit and split shell commands – These two utility commands allow a large file to be separated into several smaller files. The primary usefulness of these utilities is in the automatic naming of the individual small files created by this process. We discuss the split utility first.

The most common use of the split utility is to separate the large file into pieces based on matching a particular pattern. The pattern is to be thought of as a separator or delimiter, marking the start of a new area of interest in the large file. The default action for the split utility is that it separates a large file into files consisting of 1000 lines each, with the last file shorter if necessary. (A smaller file size can be selected using the -b option.) The files are all created with simple, easy to remember, names based on the name of the large file to be split. Unfortunately, selecting a size sometimes conflicts with the pattern matching.

The csplit utility goes a bit farther than split in that it allows the use of a regular expression rather than requiring a fixed pattern as the separator or delimiter. (The name "csplit" comes from the term "context split.") The pattern must be what is known as a "regular expression." As an example of a regular expression, we could look for any three consecutive upper case letters as a separator or delimiter by using the regular expression [A-Z][A-Z][A-Z]. For more information on what constitutes a regular expression consult any book on compiler writing or comparative computer languages.

USAGE:

csplit file_name regular_expression

split -p "ABC" file_name

34. head

Syntax: head [-n count | -c bytes] [file ...]

head shell command – The head shell command shows the first few lines in a file.

USAGE:

head file_name

35. tail

Syntax: tail [-F | -f | -r] [-q] [-b number | -c number | -n number] [file ...]

tail shell command – The tail shell command is the opposite of the head command. It shows shows the last few lines in a file.

USAGE:

tail file_name

36. tar, ar, bar, rar, gzip, gunzip, zcat

Syntax: tar [bundled-flags <args>] [<file> | <pattern> ...]

or

tar {-c} [options] [files | directories]

or

tar {-r | -u} -f archive-file [options] [files | directories]

or

tar {-t | -x} [options] [patterns]

or

ar -d [-TLsv] archive file ...

or

ar -m [-TLsv] archive file ...

or

ar -m [-abiTLsv] position archive file ...

or

ar -p [-TLsv] archive [file ...]

or

ar -q [-cTLsv] archive file ...

or

ar -r [-cuTLsv] archive file ...

or

ar -r [-abciuTLsv] position archive file ...

or

ar -t [-TLsv] archive [file ...]

or

ar -x [-ouTLsv] archive [file ...]

or

gzip [-acdfhlLnNrtvV19] [-S suffix] [name ...]

or

gunzip [-acfhlLnNrtvV] [-S suffix] [name ...]

or

zcat [-fhLV] [name ...]

tar shell command – The tar shell command manages what was once called a tape archive but now can refer to any type of archive. The most common options are the 'c' option to create an archive and the 'x' option to extract files from an existing archive. In many cases I like to use the 'v,' or verbose, option to see what files are in the archive. Other archiving commands have similar, but not identical, function and syntax.

USAGE:

tar -cf file_1 file_2 ... file_n archive

tar -xf archive

gzip files_or_directories

gunzip archive

37. cpio

Syntax: cpio {-i} [options] [pattern ...] [< archive]

or

cpio {-o} [options] < name-list [> archive]

or

cpio {-p} [options] dest-dir < name-list

cpio shell command – This shell command is a useful utility that can be used to copy files between archives and directories. The unusual name is an acronym for copy IO. The Apple Darwin implementation of this utility can extract from tar, pax, cpio, zip, jar, ar, and ISO 9660-compliant CD-ROM images and can create tar, pax, cpio, ar, and shar archives. Most UNIX users will need to use both the archiving commands such as tar, bar, ar, gzip, and gunzip, as well as cpio on occasion.

USAGE:

ls | cpio -pd destination

38. ftp

Syntax: ftp [-46AadefginpRtvV] [-N netrc] [-o output] [-P port] [-q quittime] [-s srcaddr] [-r retry]

[-T dir,max[,inc]] [[user@]host [port]] [[user@]host:[path][/]] [file:///path]

[ftp://[user[:password]@]host[:port]/path[/][;type=X]] [http:/[user[:password]@]host[:port]/path] [...]

or

ftp -u URL file [...]

ftp shell command – The ftp shell command (the name stands for file transfer protocol) is used to upload files to, and download files from, a remote server. In the author's experience, using the ftp command from a terminal window is the most reliable means of communication for transmitting one or more files to a remote host. Many programs that have more user-friendly features than the pure ftp shell command program often have conflicts with certain remote sites. In practice, relatively few of the options are used, with such activities as the entering of a password generally done within a running ftp program after a connection is created between client and host.

USAGE:

ftp host

39. ping

Syntax: ping [-AaCDdfnoQqRrv] [-b boundif] [-c count] [-G sweepmaxsize] [-g sweepminsize] [-h sweepincrsize]

[-i wait] [-l preload] [-M mask | time] [-m ttl] [-P policy] [-p pattern] [-S src_addr] [-s packetsize]

[-t timeout] [-W waittime] [-z tos] host

or

ping [-AaDdfLnoQqRrv] [-b boundif] [-c count] [-I iface] [-i wait] [-l preload] [-M mask | time] [-m ttl]

[-P policy] [-p pattern] [-S src_addr] [-s packetsize] [-T ttl] [-t timeout] [-W waittime] [-z tos]

mcast-group

ping shell command – The ping shell command is extremely useful in determining if there is a problem connecting the local machine to a network. The idea is to examine the connection to a remote machine whose static IP address is known. With no options set, the ping command attempts to send a small number of packets to the remote machine, and reports on how many of these packets were returned within a predetermined time limit. If the packets were transmitted and returned properly, then a physical connection between the host and the client computer has been proved to have been available.

USAGE:

ping remote_machine_IP_address

40. rlogin, telnet

Syntax: rlogin [-468DEd] [-e char] [-i localname] [-l username] [username@]host rlogin shell command – The rlogin shell command allows a user to connect to a remote machine on which he or she has access rights. This command may be removed in future releases of several UNIX variants and replaced by the telnet shell command.

Syntax: telnet [-468EFKLNacdfruxy] [-S tos] [-X authtype] [-e escapechar] [-k realm] [-l user] [-n tracefile] [-s src_addr] [host [port]]

telnet shell command – The telnet shell command allows a user to connect to a remote machine on which he or she has access rights. As stated above, this command may replace the rlogin shell command in future releases of several UNIX variants.

USAGE:

rlogin hostname

or

telnet hostname

41. passwd

Syntax: passwd [-i infosystem [-l location]] [-u authname] [user]

passwd shell command – The passwd shell command allows a user to change his or her password. Unlike several currently popular software applications on a variety of devices, nearly any length string of nearly any type of printable characters can be used as part of a user's password.

USAGE:

passwd

42. sh, csh, ksh, bash, posix shells

Syntax: sh

or

csh

or

ksh

or

bash

or

posix

sh, csh, ksh, bash, and posix shell selection commands – These five shell commands each create a new UNIX shell with the chosen command processor. When the new shell is terminated (by entering a CTRL-D, for example) control reverts to the original shell. This can be useful for running particular applications that were created in the specific shell selected.

We will show the major features of the C, bash, and Bourne shells and their differences. However, it is important to note that the similarities of the shells are great; the shells have much more in common than they have differences. In particular, the running of application programs, shell processes, and utilities is similar in the two shells.

The bash and Bourne shells have the easiest facilities for loops. They allow the user to control loops using the simple "for-loop" syntax that we saw earlier.

The Bourne shell is well-suited to running simple commands and simple programming. It does not allow the user to recover earlier actions such as recalling previous commands by referring to them by number. This facility is available in the C shell in the history variable that we will study later. A large amount of retyping is necessary when using the Bourne shell, unless we have a windowing system in which commands can be copied using the mouse and placed wherever needed.

The difference between the two shells that is most obvious to a casual user is the standard prompt. Unless the user changes the value of the prompt string, the prompt for the Bourne shell will be a dollar sign '$' and the C shell prompt will be a percent sign '%'. Other differences are more fundamental.

There are some program development features that are powerful and easily accessed in the C shell but are not present in the Bourne shell.

The most immediately useful feature of the C shell is the use of the history utility. This utility is initialized by a C shell command that sets the size of a buffer that will store the last few commands entered by the user. The C shell syntax is

```
set history=some_integer
```

that fixes the size of the history buffer to the specified integer. This command can be entered by the user at any time; however, it is more common to have it included in the user's .profile file so that this utility is automatically started when the user logs onto the computer. After setting the value of the history parameter, every command that is entered has a unique positive integer associated with it as an index. Assignments in the C shell are performed using the set construction.

The history utility is used to eliminate retyping long commands. Suppose you have typed several long and complicated commands such as

```
ls $HOME/source_code/*.c |wc -l sort -n
```

and that you are tired of retyping commands that you have already run. If you know the number of the previous command that you wish to retype, you can recall the command from the buffer and execute the command by typing the simple expression of an exclamation point '!' followed by the command number as in

```
!command_number
```

The exclamation point is used to tell the C shell that it should search the history buffer for the command with the index that is the integer that follows the exclamation point.

Suppose that you are unsure of the index of the command that you wish to recall. Suppose that the current command number is 126 and that the command that we want to use is number 100 (which we have forgotten). There are three choices:

1. Get a list of commands in the buffer by typing history. Check that the command is number 100 and then type !100 at the command line prompt.
2. Go backwards in the buffer using a command like

   ```
   !-offset
   ```

   that recalls a command based on its offset index from the current command. In this case, the offset would be 126 –100, or 26.
3. Match by the first character by typing !ch, where ch is the first character or set of characters that were used in the command to be recalled. In this command, it would be !l. This can be dangerous if there are other commands with similar starting characters between the current command and the desired command in the buffer.

As we have seen, the assignment of values to shell variables is different in the two shells. In the Bourne shell, a simple assignment statement suffices; thus

PS1="MY COMPUTER-->"

is adequate to change the major prompt string in the Bourne shell. Changing the prompt in the C shell involves using the set construction and looks something like

set prompt="MY COMPUTER-->"

Each of the shells allows the automatic parsing of command-line arguments and the use of shell variables. For example, a command line such as

cp file1 file2

is automatically parsed into three separate tokens. These tokens are, by convention, separated into temporary variables named

$0

for the name of the copy utility cp,

$1

for the name of the first file file1, and

$2

for the name of the second file file2, etc. The number of command line tokens is denoted by $# in both the Bourne and C shells.

USAGE:

Enter the name of the desired shell on a command line.

43. who, whoami, whois

Syntax: who [-abdHlmpqrsTtu] [file]

or

whoami

or

whois [-aAbdgiIlmQrR6] [-c country-code | -h host] [-p port] name ...

who shell command – The who shell command indicates which users are logged onto a multi-user system. It can be useful in determining if a user is still active on the system, since there is an option to list the amount of idle time, presuming that idle time means inactivity.

whoami shell command – The whoami shell command allows the user to determine which name he or she is logging in as. This is especially useful if the user has complete administrative privileges on the computer and wishes to separate what he or she does as the system administrator, root, from what he or she does as an ordinary user. (This is good practice from a security perspective, and can be extremely helpful in seeing how applications behave under the control of ordinary users instead of root.)

whois shell command – The whois shell command is used primarily to determine information about specific IP addresses and system administrators in remote machines.

USAGE:

who

whoami

whois some_IP_address

44. kill

Syntax: kill [-s signal_name] pid ...

or

kill -l [exit_status]

or

kill -signal_name pid ...

or

kill -signal_number pid ...

kill shell command – The kill shell command is used to kill a process. This means that the execution of the process is terminated, and that the entry for the process in the "process ID table" is removed, so that the UNIX process scheduler no longer attempts to provide the process with access to the CPU (or to a core, in the case of multicore computers). The process to be killed is accessed by its process ID. Processes can be killed by specific signals, each of which has particular options and actions. See the file signal.h for more information on signals. Please note that some processes are set to ignore many types of signals; signal number 9, known as KILL or SIG_KILL, cannot be ignored

A user can kill essentially any process that he or she owns, with the exception of processes with ID 0 or 1. Only a superuser can send a kill signal to a process owned by a user other than himself or herself.

USAGE:

kill pid

45. touch

Syntax: touch [-A [-][[hh]mm]SS] [-acfhm] [-r file] [-t [[CC]YY]MMDDhhmm[.SS]] file ...

touch shell command – The default action of the touch shell command is used to set the date and time of the last access and modification of a file to the current date and time. This action is especially useful when used in conjunction with the make or nmake utility. Changing the time of last modification on a file using the touch command then forces the file to be recompiled by the appropriate use of make or nmake.

USAGE:

touch file_name

46. uname

Syntax: uname [-amnprsv]

uname shell command – The uname shell command provides information on the type of hardware, the name of the machine (considered as a node in the local network), the operating system version and similar.

USAGE:

uname

47. wc

Syntax: wc [-clmw] [file ...]

wc shell command – The wc shell command counts the number of words, characters, and lines in a file. The default is to print all of these. The count of the number of lines and words is, of course, meaningless when applied to a binary file. The wc command can accept a single file, multiple files, and wildcards as arguments.

USAGE:

wc file_name

wc -l file_name

wc -c file_name

wc -w file_name

48. nslookup

Syntax: nslookup [-option] [name | -] [server]

nslookup shell command – The nslookup command searches a fundamental service of the Internet: it searches domain name servers about network hosts and domains. The command can be used in one of two modes: interactive and non-interactive. The non-interactive mode is simplest and so we discuss it first.

Non-interactive mode is used when the name or Internet address of the host to be looked up is given as the first argument. The optional second argument specifies the host name or address of a name server. The output of a non-interactive call to nslookup is specific to the optional hostname or IP address.

The syntax description of nslookup for non-interactive mode is simple:

nslookup hostname

nslookup IP_address

An interactive nslookup session allows one or more of the following potential options: server domain, server domain, root, finger, ls, view, help, ?, exit, set. You should be aware that many implementations of nslookup may not allow all of the above options.

USAGE:

nslookup hostname

nslookup IP_address

49. man

Syntax: man [-acdfFhkKtwW] [--path] [-m system] [-p string] [-C config_file] [-M pathlist] [-P pager] [-B browser] [-H htmlpager] [-S section_list] [section] name ...

man shell command – The man shell command provides access to the *man* pages. The term is short for manual and the original intent was to provide on-line manuals for the most important commands in UNIX systems. The output is generally formatted to standards of organization, which describe which words are presented in bold, which words are in italics, and what indentations should be provided. The man pages are kept in a collection of directories that at one time had been placed in either the /etc or /usr/etc directories; this has been changed and, for example, on my MacBook Air running Darwin, the man pages are stored in the directory /usr/share/man.

The man pages are grouped into a set of subdirectories. On my MacBook Air system running the Darwin version of Linux, these subdirectories are named man1, man2, man3, man4, man5, man6, man7, man8, man9, and mann.

Some UNIX commands are listed in multiple directories because the commands have different functions in different contexts. You can see which context applies if the man pages have several listings for commands with the same name, but use a description with a character in parentheses. For example, the mkdir command discussed in this book has two distinct entries in the man pages, one in the directory man1 and the other in the directory man2. Their brief description provided by the whatis command (the next shell command discussed in this book) is given here:

mkdir(1) - to make directories

mkdir(2) - to make a directory file

The default of the man command is to first examine the man1 directory and produce the information there on the terminal screen. To see the man page for another directory, such as for the command mkdir(2) in the man2 directory, enter the shell command

man 2 mkdir

which displays the information for the mkdir command described in the directory man2.

Man pages often require that a text formatting system such as troff (for text runoff) has already been installed. Even though most UNIX systems have their own local version of the man pages, rather than relying on a man pages server, this troff dependency is in the process of being superseded somewhat by html output for use by browsers.

USAGE:

man UNIX_command

man some_integer_indicating_a_manpage_directory UNIX_command

50. whatis

Syntax: whatis UNIX_command

whatis shell command – The whatis shell command provides a much shorter description of the contents of the man pages than what is normally provided by the man shell command. It is useful if you are not sure which command to use and find the man pages a bit too complicated or too time consuming to search. It is also useful if you are not sure of the spelling of a command such as creat or passwd.

USAGE:

whatis keyword

51. logout

Syntax: logout

logout shell command – This command does what you expect it to do, it logs a user out.

USAGE:

logout

COMMANDS THAT A SYSTEMS PROGRAMMER WILL FIND ESPECIALLY USEFUL

52. setuid(), seteuid()

Syntax:

```
#include <syst/types.h>
#include <unistd.h>
int setuid(uid_t uid);
or
int  seteuid(uid_t euid);
```

setuid() and seteuid() system calls – These two system calls set the values of the user ID and effective user ID, respectively. The user ID, usually written uid, is essentially the user's login name. The effective user id, euid for short, reflects new permissions that may be assigned to a process on a per-process basis. The most common uses of these system calls are for the super-user to set the euid as an ordinary user within a program, to see how the program would behave for a user who was not a super-user, and, in some cases, to allow an ordinary user with super-user privileges to upgrade access. Two related system calls, setgid() and setegid() are discussed below in item 54.

NOTE: In some Linux systems, setuid() uses the _POSIX_SAVED_IDS feature of POSIX. Thus, a setuid() (other than root) program can drop all of its user privileges, do some un-privileged work, and then revert to the original euid securely.

USAGE:

setuid(some_user_id);

seteuid(some_user_euid);

53. getuid(), geteuid()

Syntax:

uid_t getuid(void); <unistd.h>

or

uid_t geteuid(void);

getuid() and geteuid() system calls – These system calls return the uid and euid of the calling process, respectively. There are two related system calls, getgid() and getegid(), that are discussed below in item 55.

USAGE:

uid_t getuid();

uid_t geteuid();

54. setgid(), setegid()

Syntax: int setgid(gid_t gid); <unistd.h>

or

int setegid(gid_t egid);

setgid() and setegid() system calls – These two system calls behave the same as the setuid() and seteuid() system calls, except that they change the *group* ID instead of a *user* ID.

USAGE:

setgid(gid_t gid);

setegid(gid_t egid);

55. getgid(), getegid()

Syntax:

int getgid(void);   <unistd.h>

int getegid(void);

getgid() and getegid() system calls – These two system calls behave the same as the getuid() and geteuid() system calls, except that they produce the *group* ID instead of a *user* ID.

USAGE:

uid_t getgid();

uid_t getegid();

56. newgrp

Syntax: newgrp [-l] [group]

newgrp shell command – The newgrp shell command is used for creating a new group of users. Often, this is done if a new project requires a dedicated group. Placing all necessary users in the same group allows the simple setting of access permissions (rwx) at group level to allow an entire project team to view all necessary documents. Creating a new group and placing users in it does not affect any other group that these users belong to.

USAGE:

newgrp group_name

57. chroot

Syntax: chroot [-u -user] [-g -group] [-G -group,group,...] newroot [command]

chroot shell command – The chroot shell command is often used in connection with the newgrp command to allow group members to temporarily change the effective root directory to one that is desired by the group. This command is not recommended for new UNIX users or for inexperienced system administrators. See the man page for the chroot command for more information and some potential pitfalls.

USAGE:

chroot -u user_name newroot_directory

chroot -g group_name newroot_directory

58. getopt, getopt()

Syntax for the getopt shell command:

args=`getopt optstring $*` ; errcode=$?; set -- $args

getopt shell command – The getopt shell command allows the parsing of a command line to determine the value of various command-line arguments to complex commands that may be presented in multiple ways by users. For example, the chroot command described above has a -u option, a -g option, a more complex -G option, a value present for the newroot and a final, optional, command. Just determining the white space can be difficult. This command is one of the few whose man page consists primarily of a complicated example, together with caveats for the prospective user.

The highly complex getopt() function is discussed in Appendix 2 along with other important C functions.

USAGE:

See the example in the man page for the getopt shell command, *man getopt.*

COMMANDS A SYSTEM ADMINISTRATOR WILL FIND ESPECIALLY USEFUL

59. od

Syntax: od [-aBbcDdeFfHhIiLlOosvXx] [-A base] [-j skip] [-N length] [-t type] [[+]offset[.][Bb]] [file ...]

od shell command – This command creates an "octal dump" of a file. That is, it creates a translation of a file into the octal encoding of the file's contents. This encoding allows the user to see what the contents of a file actually are, even if the file is a binary file.

USAGE:

od file_name |more

60. mount

Syntax: mount

or

mount [-adfruvw] [-t lfs | external_type]

or

mount [-dfruvw] special | node

or

mount [-dfruvw] [-o options] [-t lfs | external_type] special node

mount shell command – The mount shell command mounts a file system on a specific place in a directory tree on the computer on which the user is logged in, or on a remotely connected node for which the user has permissions to mount a disk in a specific place. A remote node is linked via a mount command using the remote_host: path syntax. For security reasons, only the super-user can execute this command. Read the man pages for more information.

USAGE:

mount

mount -w file_system node

61. umount

Syntax: umount [-fv] special | node

or

umount -a | -A [-fv] [-h host] [-t type]

umount shell command – This shell command (which obviously should be spelled unmount) reverses the mounting of a file system. As was the case with mount, only the super-user can execute this command.

USAGE:

umount -f special node

62. restore, dump

Syntax: complex, not given here.

restore shell command – This is a command that does what its name suggests - it restores files from a dump of files to a tape that was created using the dump shell command. The restore and dump commands have been superseded, at least to a degree, by other archiving commands.

USAGE:

The syntax can be complex, especially for the restore shell command.

63. shutdown

Syntax: shutdown [-] [-h [-u] | -r | -s | -k] [-o [-n]] time [warning-message ...]

shutdown shell command – This command is used by the super-user in his or her administrative capacity to provide a message to warn all users to log off before the system will shut down either at a specific time or immediately. It is important to provide this information, because the reading and writing of files to and from a disk on UNIX systems is not instantaneous, and often the synchronization of data between memory buffers and the disk is delayed by as much as 30 seconds. This delay in synchronization of memory buffers and disk is due to an essential operating system design; the delays were deliberately included in UNIX to improve overall disk reading and writing performance from the perspective of total throughput.

Of course, this command is not necessary on single-user workstations, where the user is almost certainly the system administrator who ought to know if he or she intends to shut down the computer. Only the super-user can execute this command.

USAGE:

shutdown "The system will be shut down at 3:00. Please log off now to avoid losing your work."

64. lpstat

Syntax: lpstat [-E] [-H] [-U username] [-h hostname[:port]] [-l] [-W which-jobs] [-a [destination(s)]] [-c [class(es)]] [-d] [-o [destination(s)]] [-p [printer(s)]] [-r] [-R] [-s] [-t] [-u [user(s)]] [-v [printer(s)]]

lpstat shell command – The lpstat shell command provides information on the total number of print jobs that are queued up in the system. Options allow a super-user acting as system administrator to monitor long print queues and examine large jobs (such as, perhaps, those created by novice users attempting to print executable files).

When run with no arguments, lpstat will list only those jobs that have been queued by the current user. Hence, this is the most likely manner in which lpstat will be used by an ordinary user.

USAGE:

lpstat

65. rcp

Syntax: rcp [-46p] source_file target_file

or

rcp [-46pr] source_file ... target_directory

rcp shell command – The rcp shell utility behaves in essentially the same way as the cp command when copying files except, of course, that files can be copied to a remote machine. Each source_file, target_file, or target_directory argument is either a remote file name of the form "ruser@rhost:path", or a local file name.

There are a few restrictions on syntax. A local file name cannot contain the ':' character, nor can it contain an occurrence of the '/' character that appears before any usage of the ':' character.

USAGE:

rcp source_file
ruser@who_knows_where.com:/usr/me/target_name

or

rcp source_file who_knows_where.com:/usr/target_name

66. rcmd

Syntax: #include <unistd.h>

int rcmd(char **ahost, int inport, const char *locuser, const char *remuser, const char *cmd, int *fd2p);

rcmd() system call – This extremely complex system call allows the execution of a command on a remote machine. Only the super-user can execute this command. Related commands are: rresvport(), iruserok(), ruserok(), rresvport_af(), and iruserok_sa().

USAGE: See the man pages for more explanation of this command and related commands. See also the discussion of Remote Procedure Call (RPC) later in this book in item 100.

67. ps

Syntax: ps [-AaCcEefhjlMmrSTvwXx] [-O fmt | -o fmt] [-G gid[,gid...]] [-g grp[,grp...]] [-u uid[,uid...]]

[-p pid[,pid...]] [-t tty[,tty...]] [-U user[,user...]]

or

ps [-L]

ps shell command – This command is used to examine the number of processes in a system at several levels of detail. The processes examined can be restricted to the set of your processes that you are aware of directly creating, or to the set of processes that either you created directly or the operating system created for you, or, the set of all processes in the system, regardless of which user created them (which can be useful for system administrators in multi-user systems).

USAGE: ps -edalf provides a long description of processes, including the process ID. When I ran this on my MacBook Air running Darwin, it printed four entries, two for user ID 501 (me) and 2 for user ID 0. Three of the process IDs listed were in sequence, 202, 203, and 205 on my system at the time when I ran this command.

The ps -ax command provided different information on a far larger number of processes, 65, almost none of which were knowingly directly created by the user (me). The first entry was for the process with process ID 1, called /sbin/launchd on this system.

Finally, the simple ps command, without arguments, simply listed the shell process used to control and interpret the user's commands entered in a terminal window, as in

```
  PID TTY           TIME CMD
 2000 ttys000    0:00.25 -bash
```

68. ipcs

Syntax: ipcs [-abcMmopQqSsTt]

ipcs shell command – The ipcs shell command reports on the status of three types of interprocess communication (ipc) in the operating system: shared memory regions, message queues, and semaphores. Information produced includes the type of ipc data structure; the id for the ipc structure; the key used to create the structure in a call to any of the system calls shmget(), msgget(), or semget(); the mode; the owner; and the owner's group. The shmget() interprocess communication system call is is discussed in item 89; the msgget() system call is discussed in item 93; and the semget() system call is discussed in item 97.

Even on multi-user systems with many simultaneous users, it is probably easier to use this shell command without any arguments rather than trying to understand its syntax.

USAGE:

ipcs

System Calls a Systems Programmer or System Administrator Will Find Especially Useful

69. nice()

Syntax: nice [-n increment] utility [argument ...]

nice() system call – The nice() system call is used to affect the scheduling of a process. Because the utility of this function is somewhat tricky to understand, we include some of the discussion from Chapter 6, Section 5 of my book, *Advanced Topics in UNIX, Second Edition.*

It is natural to ask how an ordinary user's process can get more access to the CPU with such a scheduling algorithm. CPU access is allocated by an algorithm that uses two inputs: a dynamically determined priority and a single, relatively static base priority. For historical reasons based on the mathematical formula for the dynamically determined priority (which won't be discussed here in this book) a lower priority number means greater allocation of the CPU to a process!

A user has no real control of the computation of the dynamic priority, other than in the structure and CPU needs of his or her program. The most obvious choice to improve CPU access is to lower the base priority. There is a system call to do this: nice().

The nice() system call allows a process to change its base priority (in UNIX terminology the nice value). Its syntax is

```
nice(value);
```

The nice value can be any integer value in the range from -19 to 20. (The range is -20 to 20 on Apple Darwin.) Obviously, a lower nice value is better than a higher one for increasing CPU access. Unfortunately for the ordinary user, only the super-user can decrease the nice value of a process that is running. Ordinary users don't often use the nice() system call, since it actually reduces possibility of the process that uses it getting access to the CPU.

It is often possible to improve the performance of a set of processed that run concurrently. The measure of performance easiest to improve is the average wait time, although other measures could be improved also.

Suppose that we have profiled each process in the set for a number of inputs believed to be similar to the actual behavior of the system in normal operation. We can order the processes by the percentage of time that they spend doing disk operations or interactive I/O. Clearly processes that spend much of their time performing these types of operations are spending relatively little of their time making use of the CPU. This observation is the key to this strategy.

We can raise the nice value of the disk or I/O intensive processes by inserting the statement:

```
nice (n);
```

where n is a positive integer. This strategy will increase the dynamically-computed value of the priority of those processes. Since a high value for the dynamically-computed priority means less likelihood of obtaining access to the CPU by the most common scheduling algorithms, this will provide more opportunity for the CPU intensive processes to have access to the CPU. Note that the throughput of the disk or I/O intensive processes will not be affected significantly.

The performance of the set of processes can be improved further by choosing the integer n that serves as the argument to nice() in a judicious manner. By selecting constant values (in the range 1..20) according to the percentage of disk or I/O use, the performance can be improved.

One last observation is in order concerning this problem. If we understand each of the processes in the set of processes well enough to determine the portions that are not CPU-intensive, we can place the nice() statements at several different places to provide the maximum level of optimization. This may not be worth the trouble, especially since only the super-user can <u>decrease</u> the nice value of a process (thereby increasing its chances of getting access to the CPU)

USAGE: nice(int n);

70. socket()

Syntax: #include <sys/types.h>

#include <sys/socket.h>

int socket(int domain, int type, int protocol);

socket() system call – The socket() system call is the first of five system calls that operate on a form of interprocess communication that can work for processes on the same or different computers – sockets. The system calls are over twenty years old, have had few, if any, changes, and still form the backbone of network communication – quite a tribute to their original designers. The other system calls are bind(), listen(), accept(), and connect(); these system calls are discussed in items 71-74 below.

Four of these system calls can be used in the following steps to create a sequential server. Concurrent servers are similar, but will not be discussed here. See *Advanced Topics in UNIX, Second Edition* for more information.

- Create a socket with socket().
- Initialize a pointer and the contents of the sockaddr structure.
- Bind a name to the socket using bind().
- Use listen() to tell the kernel that we are a server process.
- Use an infinite loop to take requests using the accept() system call and new, temporary socket ids.
- Provide for cleanup after completion.

(The client will use the connect() system call, which we discuss later.)

The arguments of the socket() system call are used as follows.

- The first argument, domain, is an integer that is defined in the header file socket.h and is often one of the values AF_INET or AF_UNIX, denoting either the Internet or UNIX domains. Other domains are possible.
- The second argument, type, is also an integer that is one of the options specified in the file socket.h. The most common types of sockets are: SOCK_STREAM (for a stream socket used for pipes), SOCK_DGRAM (for a "datagram"), SOCK_RAW (for a raw or non-buffered device), SOCK_RDM (for a reliably-delivered message), and SOCK_SEQPACKET (for a stream of packets that are to be delivered in sequence).
- The third argument, protocol, is an integer that represents the type of protocol that is to be used with the

socket. (The need for a protocol is clear if we consider that sockets can be used to connect different machines.) A commonly used value for the protocol argument is 0, indicating that the operating system is to look up the correct protocol from the header file.

The value returned by a successful call to socket() is an int that is known as a socket descriptor. An unsuccessful call returns the value -1.

USAGE:

```
if ((fd = socket(AF_UNIX, SOCK_STREAM, 0) ) < 0 )
        {
        close(fd);
        exit(1);
        }
```

71. bind()

Syntax: #include <sys/types.h>

#include <sys/socket.h>

int bind(int socket_id, struct sockaddr *sockaddr, int length) ;

bind() system call – This purpose of the bind() system call is to assign a name to an existing socket that does not yet have a name.

The meaning of the first argument to bind() is obvious.

The second argument to bind() is a pointer to a structured data type with two fields. The first field of the structured data type called sockaddr, is always a symbolic constant that represents what is known as the "application family." For server and client processes that reside on the same computer, the value of this constant is AF_UNIX, which is defined in the header file sys/socket.h. The type of this constant is either an int or a short int, depending on the operating system version.

(This system call is necessary since, when a socket is created with socket(), it has no name assigned.)

USAGE:

```
if (bind(fd, (struct sockaddr *) sockaddr, length ) < 0)
  {
  perror("SERVER BIND");
  if (unlink(name) < 0)
    perror("UNLINK IN SERVER");
  close(fd);
  exit(1);
  }
```

72. accept()

Syntax: #include <socket.h>

int accept(int sock_fd, struct sockaddr *client_addr, int length);

accept() system call – The purpose of the accept() system call is to provide the means of transmission between the server and the client. In the most common usage of this system call, the first argument, sock_fd, is specified as the same in a previously executed socket() system call. The other two arguments are not initialized and receive their values as a side-effect of the accept() system call. This call returns the value -1 if unsuccessful; otherwise, it returns a positive int.

USAGE:

```
if (( temp_id = accept(fd, (struct sockaddr *) client_addr,
length ) ) < 0)
          {
          perror("ACCEPT IN SERVER");
          exit(1);
          }
```

73. listen()

Syntax: #include <socket.h>

int connect(int socket_id, int socket_id, struct sockaddr *address, int length);

listen() system call – The listen() system call allows a server process to listen for data from clients using the listen() system call:

listen(int socket_id, int MAX__ATTEMPTS);

The maximum value of MAX_ATTEMPTS is currently 5 on UNIX systems. It represents the number of times that the socket will try to receive a request for connection before failure. The reason for a limit is that the process attempting to communicate may have terminated unexpectedly and we might need to provide a graceful exit from the listener process.

USAGE:

```
if (listen(fd, 5 ) < 0)
   {
   perror("listen IN SERVER");
   exit(1);
   }
```

74. connect()

Syntax:

int connect(int socket_id, int socket_id, struct sockaddr *address, int length);

#include <sys/types.h>

#include <sys/socket.h>

connect() system call – The connect() system call is used to connect a socket to a server. As stated above, its syntax is

int connect(int socket_id, int socket_id, struct sockaddr *address, int length);

The third argument for the connect() system call is different depending on the computers on which the processes are run. On some computers running earlier versions of Solaris, it represents the length of the name of the second argument, which is of type

struct sockaddr *sockaddr;

On other systems, it may be of the form

struct sockaddr_un *sockaddr;

These may be equivalent, depending on the contents of the header file socket.h.

USAGE:

```
if ((temp_id = connect(fd, (struct sockaddr *) sockaddr,
length)) < 0 )
    {
    perror("CLIENT CONNECT");
    if (unlink(name) < 0)
      perror("UNLINK IN CLIENT");
```

```
fputs("EXITING CLIENT\n", stderr);
exit(1);
}
```

75. creat()

Syntax: int creat(char *, int)

creat() system call – This oddly spelled system call creates a file. The first argument is a character string of the file and the second argument is the permissions in octal. The value returned is a file descriptor.

If the user is not the super-user and the file already exists, then creat() returns -1. Hence, detection of the prior existence of a file by the return value of this system call can provide either a positive number (a file descriptor) or a negative number (an indication that the file already existed), which can act as a simple substitute for a semaphore.

Common terminology is that when programs use this technique to replace semaphores, in order to coordinate access to some shared resource, the file is called a "lock file." It is important to program defensively, to make sure that, even if the program stops unexpectedly, the lock file is removed in order to not deprive other users of the use of the shared resource.

USAGE:

```
if ((fd = creat(filename, octal_permissions)) == -1)
 error("Error_message");
```

ALTERNATIVE USAGE:

```
if ((fd = creat(filename, octal_permissions)) == -1)
 perror("Error_message");
```

76. open()

Syntax: int open(char *, int)

open() system call – This system call attempts to open a file. The first argument is a character string of the file and the second argument is the mode: one of "0," "1," or "2." The value returned is a file descriptor. The value of -1 is returned if there is an error such as the permissions being wrong, the file already existing, etc. Many programmers avoid the use of creat() and use only open(); however, this is not consistent with general usage.

USAGE:

fd = open(filename, mode);

77. close()

Syntax: int close(int)

close() system call– This system call closes a file. The argument is a file descriptor. It is an error to attempt to close a file if the file is already closed. However, the return value is rarely used in practice.

USAGE:

close(fd);

78. read()

Syntax: int read(int, char *, int)

read() system call – This system call reads from a file. The first argument indicates a file descriptor to read from; the second is a buffer location for buffered reads; and the third argument is the number of bytes that the reader requests. The return value is 0 if we read end of file, -1 if an error occurs, and a nonnegative number if the read is successful. The number of bytes that are read may be less than the number requested if there are only a few bytes remaining; this is not an error.

USAGE:

```
#define BUFFER_SIZE some_int
char buffer[BUFFER_SIZE];
num_read = read(file_descriptor, buffer, bytes);
```

79. write()

Syntax: int write(int, char *, int)

write() system call – The write() system call writes data to a file. The first argument is a file descriptor indicating where to write data to; the second is a buffer location for buffered writes; and the third argument is the number of bytes that the writer requests. The return value is 0 if we reach the end of file, -1 if an error, and a nonnegative number if the write is successful. The number of bytes that are written must be precisely the number requested; if not, an error occurs.

USAGE:

```
#define BUFFER_SIZE some_int
char buffer[BUFFER_SIZE];
num_written = write(file_descriptor, buffer, num_bytes);
```

or

```
if (num_written = write(file_descriptor, buffer, num_bytes) != num_bytes)
        perror("Wrong number of bytes written");
```

80. sleep()

Syntax: unsigned int sleep(unsigned int seconds);

sleep() system call – The sleep() system call suspends the execution of a process (or a thread) for the number of seconds specified in the argument.

I have found this very useful in coordinating processes that run at different rates. For example, while working on a problem in the use of certain special parameters to control the shape of a particular geometric object, I created a loop to print a copy of the graphical image. In each iteration of the loop, I included code to create the shape and, after the image was created and displayed on the screen, I had the entire process sleep for 30 seconds, so that the much slower printer could catch up and print the screen image. I started running the program on Friday night and came back Monday morning to have a large set of beautiful pictures I could analyze further. (I had tried the same approach the previous weekend, without the call to sleep(), and the program crashed because the I/O buffer was full and the program could not complete execution. Sometimes, a good sleep() is all you need!)

USAGE:

sleep(some_unsigned_int) ;

81. exit()

Syntax: void exit(int) std library

or

int exit(int); obsolete, std library

exit() function – This function terminates execution of the program and provides the status of the program, which is stored in the argument, to the environment. An argument of 0 indicates successful execution; any other argument is used to indicate an error. The return value should not be used, since usage of the exit() function with an int return value is obsolete.

When a process exits, it flushes all data in the open output streams, closes all open streams, and unlinks all data files.

USAGE:

exit(int_status);

82. fork()

Syntax: int fork();

fork() system call – The fork() system call has only one purpose: create another process. The term "fork" has long been used in concurrent programming terminology to denote a time when a new branch of some software system begins execution concurrently with other branches. The term is also commonly used in essentially the same way in the operating systems literature. The UNIX system call fork() does essentially the same thing by creating a new process; this new process is called a child process. (There is a related system call named clone() that is available in Linux systems.)

There are always precisely two of the user's processes involved in each successful use of the fork() system call: a parent process, that creates the new process, and a child process that is the newly-created process. The two processes then continue to execute and, generally speaking, have equal rights to the CPU's process scheduler. Note that to call fork() a "function" is somewhat of a misnomer, since the mathematical meaning of a *function* is that it returns exactly one value.

The process scheduler can distinguish between the parent and child processes created by a call to fork(). After a call to fork(), the child process receives the value 0, and the parent process receives the process id of the newly created child process. These are the two return values of fork() referred to above.

A simple example of the use of fork() is shown below:

```
#include <stdio.h>

int main(int  argc, char *argv[])

{

    puts("Begin fork test") ;

    fork() ;

    puts("End fork test") ;

}
```

This program has three lines of output! There is a single printing of the phrase "Begin fork test" before the call to fork(), and **two** printings of the phrase "End fork test," one for each process: the original parent process, and the new child process. (Theoretically, the phrases may be jumbled up because of the way the CPU scheduler might select either the parent or child process at any time. In fact, this is unlikely for this toy program, because the output is so small.)

A schematic diagram is shown in Figure 2.1.

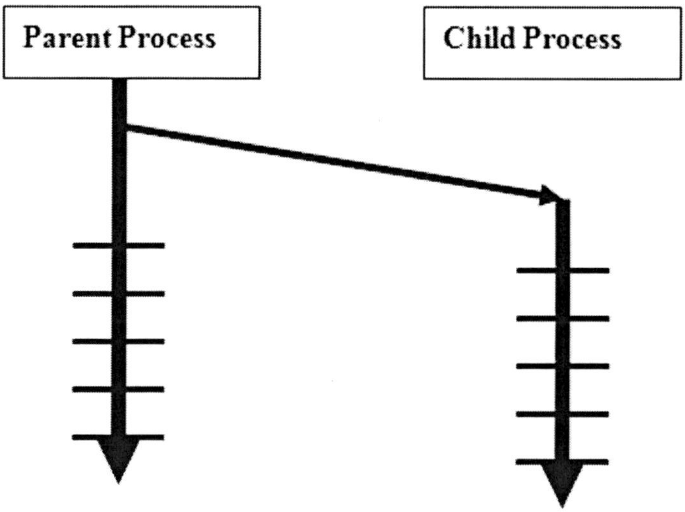

Figure 2.1 A parent creates a child process with a call to fork().

USAGE: The first example shows a simple call to fork(). The second example, shown below, illustrates how the parent and child processes created by fork() are distinguished. We will explain the execl() system call in item 83.

```
pid = fork();
```

or

```
int main(int argc, char *argv[])
{
  if (fork() == 0)  /* in child */
        execl("../count", "count",argv[1], 0);
```

```
  else /* parent process */
          printf("IN PARENT\n");
  wait(NULL);
  printf("IN PARENT, CHILD COMPLETE\n");
}
```

83. exec(), execl(), execlp(), execle(), execvp(), execve(), execvP()

Syntax: #include <unistd.h>

extern char **environ;

int execl(const char *path, const char *arg0, ... /*, (char *)0 */);

int execle(const char *path, const char *arg0, ... /*, (char *)0, char *const envp[] */);

int execlp(const char *file, const char *arg0, ... /*, (char *)0 */);

int execv(const char *path, char *const argv[]);

int execvp(const char *file, char *const argv[]);

int execvP(const char *file, const char *search_path, char *const argv[]);

exec() system calls – The family of exec() system calls all have the same purpose - to overwrite the executable code of an existing process in order to perform a desired computational task. A typical UNIX process consists of three segments: the stack segment, which keeps track of arguments to functions in a runtime stack; the data segment for the process; and the text segment, which is where the executable code lies. Technically speaking, a call to one of the exec() family of system calls overwrites the text segment of the process by that of a new process.

There are six different UNIX system calls that perform execs. We consider the simplest call, execlp(), first. An example of how this system call works is the following program.

```
#include <stdio.h>
int main(int  argc, char *argv[])
{
    puts("Hello");
    execlp("./exfile","exfile",0);
    puts("Goodbye");
}
```

Suppose that the executable file obtained by compiling and linking this program is named "doit." When doit is executed, the text segment contains the executable part of the code. The data segment contains the strings "Hello" and "goodbye," among other things.

The values of the arguments to execlp(), "./exfile," "exfile," and 0 are also in the data segment of doit. The stack segment contains appropriate shell variables and an indication that execution begins in main(). The static view of the system is described in Figure 2.2.

Now consider what happens when execution begins. The call to puts(), which is in the text segment, sends the string "Hello," which is in the data segment, to stdout. The arguments to execlp() are read from the data segment and the stack segment gets the return address for a potential return from execlp(). If we had any other function except for an exec() or similar system call, after completion of the function's execution, we would return to the address that is popped off the stack in the stack segment, and execution would continue.

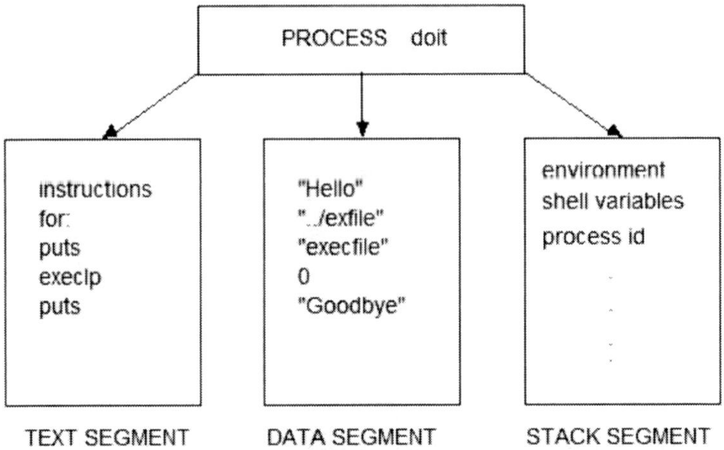

Figure 2.2 Before the call to execlp()

The system call execlp() is different from other system calls yet – it never returns to its calling routine. It cannot return, because a successful call to execlp() overwrites the segments of the process. The data segment is overwritten and the strings "Hello" and "Goodbye" and the arguments to execlp() are now gone. The executable code in the text segment of doit has been overwritten by the executable instructions in the file exfile in the parent directory. Thus the second puts() statement is never executed.

Note that the stack segment is changed to eliminate references to the return address for execlp(). See Figure 2.3. This is, of course, consistent with the inability of a return from a successful call to execlp() – there is no place to return to! Generally speaking, a call to execlp() can fail only if the executable file is not found, or if permissions are insufficient to allow execution.

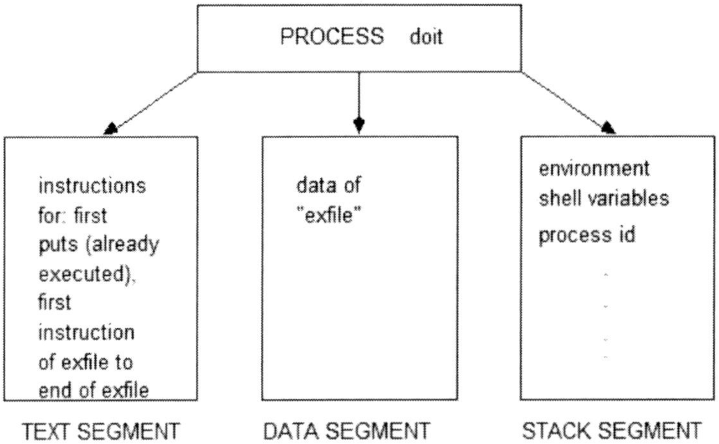

Figure 2.3 After the call to execlp()

This combination of fork()and exec() seems to be an unusual program construction. Why overwrite the segments of a process? The answer is that exec() by itself is not especially useful. The effective use of exec() is with a fork().

What is the primary difference between the different system calls in the exec() family? There are only two differences. First, and foremost, the calls execl(), execle(), and execlp() receive their command-line arguments as a list, while the other three calls, execv(), execvp(), and execvP() receive their command-line arguments in an array.

The second difference is in how the system calls react to the program environment. The execle() system call keeps the environmental variables unchanged.

USAGE:

This example shows exec'ing a process named "count" that uses its command-line argument stored in the value of argv[1].

```
int main(int  argc, char *argv[])
{
  if (fork() == 0)  /* in child */
          execl("../count", "count",argv[1], 0);
  else /* parent process */
          printf("IN PARENT\n");
  wait(NULL);
  printf("IN PARENT, CHILD COMPLETE\n");
}
```

84. thread commands

Syntax: #include <pthread.h>

int pthread_create(pthread_t *thread, const pthread_attr_t *attr, void *(*start_routine)(void *), void *arg)
Creates a new thread of execution with a function to begin executing.

int pthread_detach(pthread_t thread)   Marks a thread for deletion.

int pthread_equal(pthread_t t1, pthread_t t2)
    Compares two thread IDs.

void pthread_exit(void *value_ptr)   Terminates the calling thread.

int pthread_join(pthread_t thread, void **value_ptr) Causes the calling thread to wait for the termination of the specified thread.

int pthread_cancel(pthread_t thread) Cancels execution of a thread.

int pthread_once(pthread_once_t *once_control, void (*init_routine)(void)) Calls an initialization routine once.

pthread_t pthread_self(void) Returns the thread ID of the calling thread.

int pthread_atfork(void (*prepare)(void), void (*parent)(void), void (*child)(void)) Registers handlers to be called before and after fork()

pthread functions – This class of system calls is based on the POSIX standard and allows the creation and manipulation of threads, or lightweight processes, as opposed to the overhead of processes using fork() and exec(). (Normal UNIX processes are often called heavyweight processes when compared to threads.)

USAGE:

Threads are far too complex to discuss here. See the man pages for pthreads, the author's *Advanced Topics in UNIX, Second Edition* (available on this electronic platform) or a modern book on operating systems.

85. wait()

Syntax: #include <sys/wait.h>

pid_t wait(int *stat_loc);

or

pid_t wait3(int *stat_loc, int options, struct rusage *rusage);

or

pid_t wait4(pid_t pid, int *stat_loc, int options, struct rusage *rusage);

or

pid_t waitpid(pid_t pid, int *stat_loc, int options);

wait() system call – This system call is normally used within the parent portion of a process in which a child process is executing for synchronization purposes. When a wait() system call is used, the parent waits for a signal that the child process has terminated before continuing its execution. See the man pages for more information on the related non-standard system calls wait3() and wait4().

USAGE:

wait (int &status);

Some older programs may have been developed on legacy implementations of UNIX and may require an additional include file:

#include <sys/types.h>

86. pipe()

Syntax: int pipe(int file_descriptor[2]); #include <unistd.h>

pipe() system call – This system call sets up a pipe connection between two file descriptors that are given in an array. The int file_descriptor[0] is the read part of the pipe, while file_descriptor[1] is the write part of the pipe. See the information on pipes in Appendix 1.

USAGE:

pipe_id = pipe(int file_descriptor[2]);

87. dup()

Syntax: int dup(int fildes); #include <unistd.h>

dup() system call – The dup() system call duplicates a file descriptor. This is very useful when two processes both need to access the same file.

USAGE:

file_descriptor_1 = dup(file_descriptor_2);

88. signal() #include <signal.h>

Syntax: typedef void (*sig_t) (int);

sig_t signal(int sig, sig_t func);

signal() system call – The signal() system call allows a process to communicate with other processes. The most common setting is to have a process communicate with any of its child processes, or the reverse. When a particular signal is received, a signal handling function (of a type named sig_t in this syntax) is invoked.

There are 32 different types of signals described in the file signal.h; be aware that some older systems have a smaller number of allowable signals.

USAGE:

signal(sig_num, sig_catcher_fcn);

89. shmget()

Syntax: int shmget(key_t key, size_t size, int shmflg);

#include <sys/types.h>

#include <sys/ipc.h>

#include <sys/shm.h>

shmget() system call – The shmget() system call is a form of interprocess communication (ipc) that creates a shared memory region whose size is the second argument of the function. The return value is called the shm_ID. The region is then attached to programs if their processes if The first argument, key, is evaluated to see if a shared memory region with the same key already exists; if such a region does already exist, the call to shmget() produces an error. The shm_ID is stored "permanently" in the sense that it remains stored in a file and persists even if the processes using it terminate. The ipcs shell command indicates any shared memory regions, message queues, or semaphores.

USAGE:

shm_ID = shmget(key_t key, size_t size, int shmflg);

90. shmat()

Syntax: void * shmat(int shmid, const void *shmaddr, int shmflg);

#include <sys/types.h>

#include <sys/ipc.h>

#include <sys/shm.h>

shmat() function call – The system call shmat() is used to attach a previously created shared memory region to a process. There are two issues that a user of this system call needs to understand well: how to link the shared memory region to a process, and where to attach the region within the process. It is important to understand that what is being shared between process is a part of the data region that was shown in Figures 2.2 and 2.3.

The shmat() system call has the syntax given above. The link to the shared memory region is accomplished by the first argument, which is the shared memory ID created by a previous call to shmget().

We have now completed the first step and have created the appropriate kernel data structure. The next step is to determine safe places to attach shared memory to processes.

It is slightly complicated to find a safe place for a shared memory region in a process. By a safe place we mean a portion of shared memory that cannot be corrupted by another process using the same memory. Of course the whole point of shared memory is that two or more processes can share the same data and can read and write this data when necessary. We want the organization of the data to be interpreted the same way by all processes sharing it. Since the operating system only provides methods for reading from memory in bytes, this protection of the higher level organization of data by processes is essential.

There is some disagreement on this point. Most of the manuals suggest that the kernel be given the responsibility of finding a safe place, which corresponds to the second argument being 0 in the system call shmat() that we will meet later in this section. Stevens' text listed in the references also recommends this, but notes that there can be difficulties if there is a substantial amount of dynamic memory allocation in the process's data segment.

We illustrate the point by two examples:

```
int main(int argc, char *argv[])
{
  int i;
  float f;
  int j;
/* more code here */
}
```

and

```
int main(int argc, char *argv[])
{
  int i;
  int j;
  float f;
  /* more code here */
}
```

Assume that in each system, an integer takes 2 bytes, a floating point number takes four bytes, and that the shared memory region must stop on a word boundary (a multiple of 4 bytes). In each example, there are a total of 8 bytes in the data segment.

In the first example, a shared memory region of 4 bytes cannot be placed since its boundaries would fall in the middle of the storage of the floating point number. Any other process writing to such an area would corrupt the organization of the data.

In the second example, a shared memory region can begin at the beginning location, byte 0, or after the second integer in byte 4. Any other place would always allow the possibility of data corruption.

There is another possibility for sharing memory between processes –take an unused portion of memory. We could find the upper limit of the data segment and then anything added after this place would appear to be safe. This upper limit is called the "break value." The upper boundary of the data segment can be found by using the sbrk() system call such as

break_val = sbrk(0);

There is a problem, however. If the program uses any dynamic storage allocation, then the original size of the data segment, and hence the break value, may have been modified as the process runs. Thus any use of dynamic storage allocation whether explicitly by the user's calling of the storage allocator malloc(), or by pointers, character strings, or structured data types, requires care to make sure that the area chosen for shared memory is chosen properly.

Clearly, the decision about the place to attach a shared memory region requires extensive knowledge of the organization of the data segment of the process. All this information gathering must be done by the user, not the kernel. The next step is the attachment of the shared memory region to the processes in the previously determined places. This requires the use of the shmat() system call. The return value that is not ordinarily used except for testing success (a non-negative value) or failure (-1). Since the only use of the return value is to test for error, we need only cast the return type as an int to check for failure (return value = -1). The second argument should be set to 0, as in (char *) 0, if the kernel is to determine the place for attachment. Otherwise, user should select the place as discussed above.

USAGE:

shmat(key, 0xF0 ,SHM_RDONLY|SHM_RND);

Note that some older implementations require a different cast operation, since the original syntax was

char *shmat(int shmid, char *shmaddr, int shmflg);

91. shmdt()

Syntax: int shmdt(const void *shmaddr);

#include <sys/types.h>

#include <sys/ipc.h>

#include <sys/shm.h>

shmdt() system call – This system call detaches a shared memory region from the address space of a process. It must follow a call to shmat() with the same base address as was returned by the shmat() system call. Note that since many processes may be using the same shared memory region, a call to shmdt() does not remove the region from the kernel's shared memory table. This system call has only a single parameter which is the starting address of the process in the user's address space. Thus processes that attach several regions to the same base address may cause some problems. It is the responsibility of the user to know the place where the regions were attached. Since the system call shmdt() does not have any way of entering the size of the shared memory region, attaching shared memory regions of different size to the same place won't work..

USAGE:

shmdt(0xF0); /* This uses an argument used in a previous shmat() call. */

92. shmctl()

Syntax: int shmctl(int shmid, int cmd, struct shmid_ds *buf);

#include <sys/types.h>

#include <sys/ipc.h>

#include <sys/shm.h>

shmctl() system call – The shmctl() system controls information in a "shared memory data structure" of the following form.

```
struct shmid_ds {
    struct ipc_perm   shm_perm;          /* operation permissions */
    int          shm_segsz;    /* size of segment in bytes */
    pid_t          shm_lpid;     /* pid of last shm op */
    pid_t          shm_cpid;     /* pid of creator */
    short          shm_nattch;   /* # of current attaches */
    time_t          shm_atime;    /* last shmat() time*/
    time_t          shm_dtime;    /* last shmdt() time */
    time_t          shm_ctime;    /* last change by shmctl() */
    void          *shm_internal; /* sysv stupidity */
};
```

Note the comment by an anonymous software maintainer about the usage of the pointer to shm_internal!

USAGE:

The proper use of this system call is highly complex. For more information, please see the man pages or the author's book *Advanced Topics in UNIX, Second Edition*, which is available on this electronic platform.

93. msgget()

Syntax: #include <sys/msg.h>

int msgget(key_t msg_key, int flag);

msgget() system call – The purpose of the msgget() system call is to take its primary argument, which is called the key, and use this and the second argument, which is a flag, to return an integer called a queue_id. The queue_id returned by a successful call to msgget() is an index into the kernel's message queue data structure table; the system call returns -1 if there is an error. Multiple processes can communicate by sending and receiving messages using the same message queue. The ipcs shell command indicates any semaphores, message queues, or shared memory regions.

The return value is called the msg_ID. The type key_t of the first argument is defined in the include file sys/types.h as being of type long; the definition is made using a C language typedef construction. This is consistent with much of the older code using messages in which the type of key_t is declared as long.

The proper determination of the key argument can be a tricky business. It is important to have the reader and writer of a message queue use the same message queue; this means that they each know the same queue_id. The key can be kept relatively private by using the makekey() function that is commonly used for data encryption as the key argument. For simple programs, it is probably sufficient to use the process id of the creator process (assuming that the other processes wishing to access the message queue know this number) or even to hard code the key argument as a particular constant.

Note: The Apple Darwin version of UNIX does not include information on any of the four system calls – msgget(), msgsnd(), msgrcv(), and msgctl() – that are used with message queues. The copyrighted information about the message queue ID data structure described in the header file /usr/include/sys/msg.h is proprietary and, unfortunately, cannot be presented here. We note that there are some variables and data in this header file that are highly Apple-specific.

An older version of a message queue data structure (not the Apple Darwin version) is given below.

```
struct msqid_ds
 {
 struct ipc_perm msg_perm;   /* Permission struct. */
 struct msg      *msg_first; /* Pointer to first message.*/
 struct msg      *msg_last;  /* Pointer to last message. */
 ushort          msg_cbytes; /* Number of bytes on queue */
 ushort          msg_qnum;   /* Number of messages on queue. */
 ushort          msg_qbytes; /* Max number of bytes on queue. */
 ushort          msg_lspid;  /* pid of last msgsnd */
 ushort          msg_lrpid;  /* pid of last msgrcv */
 time_t          msg_stime;  /* last msgsnd time */
 time_t          msg_rtime;  /* last msgrcv time */
 time_t          msg_ctime;  /* last change time */
 };
```

USAGE:

msg_id = msgget(key_t key, int flag);

94. msgsnd()

Syntax: int msgsnd(int, const void *, size_t, int);

msgrcv() system call – The msgrcv() system call is used for a process receiving messages from other processes using a message queue.

USAGE:

int msgsnd(int queue_id, struct msgbuf * msg_ptr, int message_size, int flag);

95. msgrcv()

Syntax: ssize_t msgrcv(int, void *, size_t, long, int) ;

msgrcv() system call – The msgrcv() system call is used for a process sending messages to other processes using a message queue.

USAGE:

int msgrcv(int queue_id, struct msgbuf * msg_ptr, int message_size, long msgtype, int flag);

96. msgctl()

Syntax: int msgctl(int queue_id, int command, struct msqid_ds_ptr *);

msgctl() system call – The msgctl() system call controls information in a “message data structure.” This system call has three arguments, the first of which is a queue_id.

It is assumed that the queue_id exists before the call to msgctl(); otherwise the system is in an error state. Note that if the two system calls msgget() and msgctl() are called by different processes, then there is a potential for a "race condition"; that is, the result of the program depends on the execution timing of the system calls. Therefore the preferred method of designing a concurrent software system using these two system calls is to have them both included within the same process.

USAGE:

The proper use of this system call is highly complex. For more information, please see the man pages (on a non-Apple system) or the author's book *Advanced Topics in UNIX, Second Edition*, which is available on this electronic platform.

97. semget()

Syntax: int semget(key_t key, int nsems, int semflg);
#include <sys/sem.h>

semget() function – The semget() system call returns the identifier of a newly created or previously existing set of semaphores. The return value is called the sem_id. The sem_id is stored "permanently" in the sense that it remains stored in a file and persists even if the processes using it terminate. The ipcs shell command indicates any semaphores, message queues, or shared memory regions.

USAGE:

sem_id = int semget(key_t key, int num_sems, int flags);

98. semop()

Syntax: int semop(int semid, struct sembuf *sops, size_t nsops);

semop() function – The semop() function performs operations on a set of semaphores. This system call returns 0 if it generates no errors and returns -1 if the call is unsuccessful. It has three parameters: semid, sem_op, and num_ops. The first parameter is the id of the semaphore that we are operating on. If there is no semaphore with that id in the kernel's data space, then the system call returns -1.

The second parameter provides an encoding of either one of the incrementation or decrementation operations. The second parameter is always a pointer to a variable of type sembuf. There are three fields to each such semaphore data structure:

sem_num,

that is an unsigned integer (usually also a short integer);

sem_op,

that is a short integer, and

sem_flg,

which is also a short integer that is similar to the flags used with semget().

The second field sem_op of the structure is of type short integer and is interpreted as an operation on the existing semaphore value. The simplest case requires the kernel to:

increment the semaphore by x

if the parameter is a positive int x, and

decrement the semaphore by y

if the parameter is a negative int y and the result of the decrementation would still have the value of the semaphore non-negative.

USAGE: We show the typical usage of semop() by embedding semop() commands in a pair of functions named P() and V() in keeping with the classic terminology.

```
void P(int sid)    /* acquire semaphore */
{
    struct sembuf sb;
```

```
    sb.sem_num = 0;
    sb.sem_op = -1;
    sb.sem_flg = SEM_UNDO;
    if ((semop(sid,&sb,1)) == -1)
      puts("semop error");
}
void V(int sid)    /* release semaphore */
{
    struct sembuf sb;
    sb.sem_num = 0;
    sb.sem_op = 1;
    sb.sem_flg = SEM_UNDO;
    if ((semop(sid,&sb,1)) == -1)
      puts("semop error");
}
```

99. semctl()

Syntax: int semctl(int semid, int semnum, int cmd, ...);

#include <sys/sem.h>

semctl() system call – The semctl() system call controls information in a "semaphore data structure" of the following form.

struct semid_ds {

struct ipc_perm sem_perm; /* operation permission struct */

struct sem *sem_base; /* pointer to first semaphore in set */

u_short sem_nsems; /* number of sems in set */

time_t sem_otime; /* last operation time */

long sem_pad1; /* SVABI/386 says I need this here */

time_t sem_ctime; /* last change time */

/* Times measured in secs since 00:00:00 GMT, Jan. 1, 1970 */

long sem_pad2; /* SVABI/386 says I need this here */

long sem_pad3[4]; /* SVABI/386 says I need this here */

};

As was the case with the shared memory data structure, the comments written by an anonymous software maintainer about some of the data fields is illuminating when considered in light of the complexity of the semctl() system call and the related data structures.

USAGE:

The proper use of this system call is highly complex. For more information, please see the man pages or the author's book *Advanced Topics in UNIX, Second Edition*, which is available on this electronic platform.

100. Remote Procedure Call (RPC)

Syntax: #include <rpc/rpc.h>

int registerrpc(int PROG, int VERSION, int PROC_NUM, char *proc_name, arg_type *arg, return_type *return_value);

int callrpc(char *node_name, int program_number, int version_number, int procedure_number, char *type_of arg, arg_type arg, char *return_type, return_type return_value);

There are relatively few primary RPC system calls and a large number of ancillary ones. We only list the primary system calls here.

Remote Procedure Call system calls – RPC allows a process to use either the same or different computers on a network to run procedures for itself. RPC allows a client process to request information from a server process. The server process calls a procedure to perform the computation and then sends back the result of the procedure or function. (The term "procedure" is confusing in this context. Except for a few scattered instances in which there are bindings to other languages, UNIX RPC is generally implemented commercially only for C programs and there is no concept of a separate entity called procedures in C. Common usage is that C functions that do not return values are still called functions.) For simplicity, we will use the term "procedure" to mean "function" in this section.

More specifically, the server process follows the steps:

- Receive a request for a computation.
- Determine the arguments for the procedure.
- Invoke the procedure.
- Send back results.
- Wait for next message.

The client process follows the steps:

- Send information to the server about the procedure to be called and the arguments.

- Block execution and wait for the request to be serviced and data sent back.
- Continue execution.

How does this RPC method differ from the much more common call of an ordinary procedure from within a program? The main differences are:

- Parameters are passed by value since there is no way to convert addresses on one machine to addresses on another.
- The environment in which a procedure is running is not passed. Therefore global variables in the caller process are not available to the remote procedure.
- The return to the caller process will not occur if the remote procedure never terminates. The remote procedure call can also fail if there is a network transmission problem.

RPC is somewhat more general than ipc because there can be multiple types of data returned by different "procedures," instead of using a socket or other ipc mechanism to convey a stream of data of the same type.

The values of the first three arguments of the call to the function registerrpc() are generally set by the user as constants in a separate header file. The first argument, PROG, is set according to a standard convention described later in this section. The second argument is an integer denoting which version of the procedure is to be used. (This is useful if we are updating procedures in the server and don't wish to make major changes to client programs.) By convention, the number 1 is usually used for the value of the version number unless a newer version of a procedure will be replacing an older one. The third argument,

PROC_NUM, indicates which procedure in the code is to be executed. Also by convention, the NULL procedure is given version number 0, so that the value of the third argument is 1 for the first procedure used.

The fourth argument, proc_name, is the name of the procedure that is to be registered as the first argument. The last two arguments, arg and return_value, refer to the nature of the arguments and the return value of the procedure named in the argument proc_name. In order to execute a procedure, the value of proc_name might be something like "remote_users;" the type of the argument arg would be xdr_bytes (to be defined later), since this argument is a string; and the return type would be xdr_long (also to be defined later), since the library function nrusers() returns a long int.

You may have noticed that there was only a single argument for passing an actual parameter that was given to registerrpc(). (The other arguments indicate that there is a single value returned, with no side effects.) This is not an error. The convention is that RPC procedures called have only one argument and one return value, with no other variables being affected by side effects. The way to have multiple arguments or multiple side effects is to incorporate the desired variables into a single structure and pass that structure. For simplicity, we will consider only procedures with simple arguments and refer the reader to the references for more information on the more complex cases.

It also appears that we are passing arguments by reference, because of the use of pointers. This is not completely correct, since the remotely-called procedure cannot understand addresses from the caller process. The addresses are only used by registerrpc(), and not by the remotely-called procedure.

Each program can set its number directly without the use of the registerrpc() library call. In order to do this, the following convention must be observed.

Range of numbers	Usage
0 - 1fffffff	Reserved by Sun
20000000-3fffffff	User-defined
40000000-5fffffff	Temporary use
60000000-7fffffff	User-defined
80000000-9fffffff	User-defined
a0000000-bfffffff	User-defined
c0000000-dfffffff	User-defined
e0000000-ffffffff	User-defined

Use of the first group is reserved by Sun for general applications in much the same way as the assignment of Internet addresses. The second group is the most common one for new programs during debugging. This is why many published examples in the popular networking literature use the fixed number 20000000 for a procedure number, avoiding the use of the function registerrpc(). There is clear danger in programs that avoid use of registerrpc() if the network is heavily used.

We now consider data transmission. The client-server model becomes much more powerful if it allows the different computers to have different operating systems or even different architectures. This forces us to have a set of routines for translating between different forms of data representation on different computers. Most operating systems now contain a set of standard library routines to handle external data representation, or XDR. Routines are available for both encoding local data into the XDR format and for decoding data from the XDR format into the format of local data. The set of library routines is extensive and includes facilities for the following.

- Detection of the end of a logical record (Example: xdrrec_endofrecord) and the end of a file (Example: xdrrec_eof).
- Translation of standard data types (Examples: xdr_char, xdr_double, xdr_long, xdr_bytes, and xdr_boolean).
- Translation of user-defined data types such as: strings (Example: xdr_string), pointers (Example: xdr_pointer), and unions (Example: xdr_union).
- Manipulation of the "xdr stream" (Examples: xdrstdio_create and xdr_destroy).

The most essential library function for programs using the intermediate layer of RPC is callrpc() (or rpc_call()). This function is used after a successful registering of the name either by using registerrpc() or by hand. The function callrpc() returns the value 0 if it is successful and returns a negative value otherwise.

This function takes eight arguments. Its syntax is

int callrpc(char *node_name, int program_number, int version_number, int procedure_number, char *type_of arg, arg_type arg, char *return_type, return_type return_value);

The first argument is a null-terminated character string indicating the name of the node on which the procedure is to be run. The next three arguments are the program, version, and procedure numbers as in registerrpc().

The next two arguments to callrpc() indicate the type of the arguments to the remote procedure specified in the first argument. The type xdr_void is used for the fifth argument to callrpc() if there are no arguments to the remote procedure. A similar statement holds for the last two arguments to callrpc() since this is where the information about the return type of the remote procedure is stored.

We now describe the use of the RPC intermediate layer. We will need to include the header file rpc/rpc.h in each program that uses this layer of RPC. This header file contains the names of other header files for most lower-level RPC functions, so that its inclusion allows access to all standard RPC library functions.

At the intermediate levels of RPC, a server program has the form

```
create_RPC_support();
registerrpc(...);
svc_run();
if (error)
    exit();
```

USAGE:

The proper use of this system call is highly complex, and has additional complications due to the increase in secure, encrypted communication, including the DES standard. For more information, please see the man pages on your system. Be aware that you may have to look under "rpc" instead of the particular system call name on some UNIX and Linux systems.

101. **unlink**()

Syntax: int unlink(const char *); #include <unistd.h>

unlink() function -– This function removes a link to a file whose name is given as the second argument. The operation of this system call changes the count of the number of links, which is stored in the i-node table. There is no other action performed if the count of the number of links is still positive.

If the count becomes 0, reflecting that no process is accessing the file, then the file's resources, including its entries in the i-node table, are removed. This allows the disk blocks originally allocated to the file to be freed up for access by other files requiring disk storage.

As a consultant on identity theft and the author of two books on the subject, I would be remiss if I did not warn you of a potential risk to any confidential data stored on your computer. Keep in mind that the contents of the disk blocks are not overwritten at this point, leaving a security hole (because the data is still on the disk!) if some criminal hacker gets access to your computer or if you intend to recycle the computer after it becomes obsolete.

USAGE:

```
if (unlink(filename) == -1)
        perror(SOME_ERROR_MESSAGE);
```

Appendix 1: The Most Essential UNIX Files

File descriptors

UNIX and all its variants, including Linux, have two fundamental types of objects: files and processes. Simply speaking, a process is a program under execution. Anything else, including the source code and the executable code for a program, is considered a file.

From the point of view of the UNIX operating system, a UNIX file can be accessed in only one way – by using an integer called a "file descriptor." All data in a file can be written or read only by using this file descriptor.

Each UNIX process automatically has three file descriptors associated with it when the process is created. The three file descriptors, which are always numbered 0, 1, and 2, refer to stdin, stdout, and stderr, respectively. Each of these is discussed below. There is a maximum number of file descriptors that can be associated with any process, which means that there is a limit to the number of files that a process can have open while it is running. This maximum number is guaranteed to be at least 20; to make sure that your programs are portable across all UNIX variants, you should avoid using more than 20 different file descriptors in a program as much as possible.

There is often some confusion about whether files that can be accessed using "file pointers" as in a language such as C with its I/O calls to fopen(), fread(), fwrite(), and fclose()

count towards this maximum number of file descriptors per process limit. The answer is yes, because these four C functions are implemented on UNIX systems by using these function calls to call the four lower-level system calls open(), read(), write(), and close(). We repeat for emphasis that the only way to access files on UNIX systems is by using system calls, although the connection may not be evident if you are programming in a higher-level language. Refer to Figure 1.1 for more information.

stdin

As we saw above, file descriptor 0 is assigned to stdin. This term refers to standard input, such as a process getting its input from the default input device, which is the keyboard.

stdout

As we saw above, file descriptor 1 is assigned to stdout. This term refers to standard output, such as a process sending its output to the default output device, which is a display terminal.

stderr

As we saw above, file descriptor 2 is assigned to stderr. This term refers to standard error, such as a process sending its error messages to the default output device, which is also a display terminal. At first glance, this seems pointless, since the same display device gets both the regular, expected output from a process as well as any error messages. The advantage becomes obvious, however, when we learn how to redirect input and output from file descriptors, which we describe in the next section.

Redirection of input and output

Let's start by looking at the cat command. Typing the shell command

cat file_1

sends the contents of the file named file_1 to the display screen. In other words, when this shell command executes, and thereby becomes a process, its output is sent to stdout; that is, to the display terminal.

We can redirect this output to another file named, say, out_file, typing the command

cat file_1 > out_file

What is happening here? The first part of the command, cat file_1, copies the contents of the file file_1 to stdout. The second part of the command, > out_file, takes its input and sends it to the file out_file. What do you think is the input to the second part? The stdout output from the first part!

We could also send the output of a process to a file instead of to stdout by typing something like

process_1 > outfile

The power of this approach becomes apparent if you think about how little programming was needed to do this operation. We simply change the output using a single character, >. Anyone familiar with the C++ programming language will note the similarity to the >> symbol for output.

We can also redirect input. For example, suppose we wish to test the behavior of a program named "process_1" on a set of input commands that we have written. We could enter all the input commands in response to program prompts. A better way to do this is to place all the input commands in a file named, say, infile, and redirect the input to the process_1 program by simply typing

```
process_1 < infile
```

We can combine the two redirections by something like

```
process_1 < infile > outfile
```

Now, let's return to the discussion of stderr. It can sometimes be annoying to have the error messages written directly to the display screen, especially if we wanted to keep these error messages permanently in an error log. We can separate the outputs of a computation with a process called process_name, with all normal output going to the screen (or to other files if specifically set by the process) going to the display screen and stderr going to an error file by something like

```
process_name 2 > error_file
```

Notice the syntax. The number 2, of course, refers to file descriptor 2, for stderr.

Errors, errno, and perror()

A special variable is often used with UNIX programs that have error checking: errno. This variable refers to a value stored in the file errno.h, which is often included in many C programs. The syntax is something like including the following within a C program:

```
#include errno.h
extern int errno;
```

The idea is to save the programmer the effort of repeating error messages such as "Error: the file does not exist." or "Error: Access permission denied." that may occur frequently within C programs.

As an example, by setting the value of the variable errno to the symbolic constant EACCES, which is found in the errno.h file, and calling the function perror() with the argument EACCES, as in perror(EACCES), a simple error message can be printed that is consistent for each occurrence of this error.

Where do the error messages printed by perror() appear? They are printed to stderr, which is usually the display terminal.

Pipes

It is easy to connect processes so that the output of the first process is redirected to the input of a second process by using the pipe symbol, |. Here is an example of using a pipe to count the number of processes running in a system. We simply use a ps command to list all running processes, and pipe the output to the UNIX wc (word count) utility, with the -l option to count the number of lines:

```
ps -ax |wc -l
```

When I ran this command on my system, this command showed that 63 processes were running at the time I did this exercise.

There is also a pipe() system call that can perform the same action within programs. We discussed this system call previously in item 86.

The i-node table

UNIX, and all its variants, do not store information on files in a way that allows all the contents of files to be accessed directly. Access to files is done by examining entries in an array of i-nodes., which is usually stored as a contiguous set of disk blocks in a special area of the disk. The elements of the array are indexed by an int variable called an i-number. An i-node has the following contents:

- File type (ordinary, directory, or special).
- Number of links to the file.
- File owner's user ID.
- File owner's group ID.
- File access permissions.
- File size in bytes.
- Time and date of last access.
- Time and date of last modification.
- Time and date of creation.
- Pointers to logical disk blocks containing file data (or pointers) There are typically a maximum of 13 such pointers in an i-node in a standard UNIX installation,

and 15 such pointers in a a typical Linux installation. Most of the pointers point to disk blocks containing data.

There is one important thing to notice about the structure of an i-node. An i-node associated with a file does not contain the name of the file. Access to a file by using its name requires the use of directory files.

The action of going to the place on the disk where the file's data is stored may have several levels of indirection. For example, many UNIX systems allow three levels of file indirection. We show how these levels of indirection work by an example.

Suppose that our system has a block size of 1024 bytes and that each address can be stored as a 32 bit integer, each of which requires the use of 4 bytes. The 13 disk pointers stored in an i-node contain:

- 10 direct pointers
- 1 singly indirect pointer
- 1 doubly indirect pointer
- 1 triply indirect pointer

The 10 direct pointers can directly access a total of 10 disk blocks that contains a total of 10 * 1,024 or 10,240 bytes, which is adequate for very small files. The singly indirect pointer points to a disk block that contains a maximum of 1,024/4 or 256 pointers, since each pointer needs four bytes. Each of these pointers can point to a disk block containing the 1,024 bytes of data in a block. Thus single indirection increases the maximum possible size of a file by 256 * 1024 or 262,144 bytes.

For Linux systems, which contain 15 disk pointers arranged as follows, the maximum file size can be slightly larger:

- 12 direct pointers
- 1 singly indirect pointer
- 1 doubly indirect pointer
- 1 triply indirect pointer

The use of double and triple indirection greatly increases the maximum possible file size at the expense of greater time needed for file access because of the indirection. In double indirection, we have 256 pointers to disk blocks, each of which is a pointer to 256 disk blocks. Since each disk block can contain 1,024 bytes of data, there is a total of 256 * 256 * 1,024 or 67,108,864 bytes available. In triple indirection, we have 256 pointers to disk blocks, each of which is a pointer to 256 disk blocks, each of which is a pointer to 256 disk blocks, each of which can contain 1024 bytes of data for a total of 256 * 256 * 256 * 1,024 or 17,179,869,184 bytes. The total amount of data that can be stored in a file on such a system is 17,247,258,432 bytes.

The maximum size of a file is a tunable parameter that can be set by the system administrator. Many systems do not allow such large files for reasons of performance and efficient use of storage. Most storage systems do not allow file sizes to be close to this maximum limit. A limit of one or two megabytes is common for systems used primarily for teaching. Such systems have fewer than the 13 maximum possible number of pointers (15 in Linux) to disk blocks in an i-node.

As we stated in our discussion of the ls shell command, selecting the option

ls -i

prints the names of the files in the directory together with their i-numbers.

Appendix 2: The Most Essential C Functions

abs()

Syntax: int abs(int) math library.

NOTE: This function is in stdlib.h in ANSI C.

absolute value function

USAGE: int_result = abs(int_argument)

acos()

Syntax: double acos(double) math library

inverse cosine function

USAGE: double_result = acos(double_argument)

asin()

Syntax: double asin(double) math library

inverse sine function

USAGE: double_result = asin(double_argument)

atan()

Syntax: double atan(double) math library

inverse tangent function

USAGE: double_result = atan(double_argument)

atof()

Syntax: float atof(char *) std library

changes ASCII string to float

USAGE: float_result = atof(char_string)

atoi()

Syntax: int atoi(char *) std library

changes ASCII string to int

USAGE: int_result = atof(char_string)

calloc()

Syntax: (void *) calloc(int, int) std library

NOTE: Many UNIX implementations have two versions of this function. One is in the standard library and the other is in the malloc library. To use the malloc library, include the file malloc.h and compile with the -lmalloc option.

calloc() returns a pointer to a region containing precisely enough memory to hold an array. The first argument to calloc() represents the number of elements in the array and the second argument represents the size of an element in the array. The pointer is to char in Kernighan and Ritchie C and the pointer is to void in ANSI C. The two int parameters should always be positive.

USAGE: pointer = (pointer_type *) calloc(number_of_elements, element_size)

ceil()

Syntax: double ceil(double) math library

ceiling function – returns a double-precision number that is on the next integer boundary greater than or equal to the argument.

USAGE: double _result = ceil(double_argument)

cos()

Syntax: double cos(double) math library

cosine function

USAGE: double_result = cos(double_argument)

cosh()

Syntax: double cosh(double) math library

hyperbolic cosine function

USAGE: double_result = cosh(double_argument)

exp()

Syntax: double exp(double) math library

exponential function

USAGE: double_result = exp(double_argument)

fabs()

Syntax: double fabs(double) math library

floating point absolute value function

USAGE: double_result = fabs(double_argument)

fclose()

Syntax: int fclose(FILE *) stdio.h

close file function - closes the input file given in the argument,

return value of −1 for error

USAGE: fclose(file_stream)

feof()

Syntax: int feof(FILE *) stdio.h

feof function − returns 0 unless the END_OF_FILE character has been read from the input stream pointed to by the file pointer; in this case it returns a nonzero value. This is used to detect reading after the END_OF_FILE.

USAGE:
```
if ( file_error = feof(file_stream) )
        exit(file_error);
```

fflush()

Syntax: (char *) fflush(int) stdio library

flush buffer function − empties output buffers if we wish to force their output. Useful in C++ programs for synchronizing output when using both printf and cout in the same program.

USAGE: fflush(file_stream);

fgetc()

Syntax: int fgetc(int) stdio library

fgetc function − gets character from an input stream Identical to getc() in use. Somewhat slower than getc() because getc() is usually implemented as a macro.

USAGE: ch = fgetc(file_ptr);

fgets()

Syntax: (char *) fgets(int, int,int) stdio library

fgets function – gets the number of characters specified in the second argument from the input stream specified in the third argument and places them in order in the array of consecutive memory locations starting from position 0 in the array specified by the address of the first argument. A new line in the input is read into the array; this is different from the treatment of gets().

USAGE: str_ptr = fgets(starting_address, number_of_char, file_ptr)

floor()

Syntax: double floor(double) math library

floor function – returns a double-precision number that is on the next integer boundary smaller than the argument.

USAGE: double_result = floor(double_argument)

fmod()

Syntax: double fmod(double) math library

floating point mod function – returns the remainder after division of the first argument by the second, or returns 0 if division by 0

USAGE: double_result = fmod(double_arg1, double_arg2)

fopen()

Syntax: (FILE *) fopen(char *, char *) stdio library

open file function – opens the file stream given in the first argument. The second argument is one of: "r", "w", "a", "r+", "w+", or "a+". Three of the arguments refer to read, write, and append. The '+' refers to having the file open for both reading and writing and the positioning of the file pointer at the beginning or end of the file. See the man page for fopen() for more information.

USAGE: file_ptr = fopen(file_name, mode)

fprintf()

Syntax: int fprintf(int, char *, var_args) stdio library

fprintf function – prints to the file stream specified in the first argument as output. The output is formatted according to the control specifications in the second argument. The variables that get their values printed are in the remaining arguments. The usage

fprintf(stdout, control_char_string, other_args)

is equivalent to the usage

printf(control_char_string, other_args)

See also the functions printf() and scanf().

USAGE: fprintf(file_ptr, control_char_string, other args);

NOTE: The order of control specifications and arguments to be printed can be changed and any number of them can be mixed in any order.

fputc()

Syntax: int fputc(char, FILE *) stdio.h

fputc function – writes its first argument to the output stream specified by the second argument, which is a pointer to a FILE. The return value is the int equivalent of the first argument. See also the function putc(), which has the equivalent action.

USAGE: int_val = fputc(ch, file_ptr);

fputs()

Syntax: int fputs(char *, FILE *) stdio.h

fputs function – takes the first argument, which is a character string, and places it on the output stream specified in the second argument. The first argument must be terminated by a null byte; this null byte is not written to the output stream. See also puts().

USAGE: int_val = fputs(char_ptr, file_ptr);

free()

Syntax: void free(void *) std library

free function – releases a memory region previously allocated by a call to malloc() or calloc().

USAGE: free(void_ptr);

fscanf()

Syntax: int fscanf(FILE *, char*, var_args) stdio library

fscanf function – reads from the input stream specified in the first argument according to the control specifications in the second argument. The variables that get assigned values are in the remaining arguments.

USAGE: fscanf(file_ptr, control_char_string, other args);

fseek()

Syntax: int fseek(FILE*, long int. int) stdio.h

fseek function – allows random access to a file pointed to by the first argument. The second argument is used as the file offset from the current position, which is specified in the third argument.

USAGE: fseek(file_ptr, file_offset, current_position);

getc()

Syntax: int getc(char*) stdio library

get character from an input stream

USAGE: ch = getc(file_ptr);

getchar()

Syntax: int getchar(void) stdio library

get character from standard input. This is the equivalent of getc(stdin);

USAGE: ch = getchar();

getopt()

Syntax for the getopt() function #include <unistd.h>

```
extern char *optarg;
extern int optind;
extern int optopt;
extern int opterr;
```

```
extern int optreset;

int getopt(int argc, char * const argv[], const char
*optstring);
```

getopt() C function – This C function interfaces to the command line, which is processed by the shell on UNIX systems. The variables optarg, optind, optopt, opterr, and optreset are declared as being external to the program in which getopt() is used. The values of these variables are provided to the program by the shell.

USAGE: See the example in the man page, man 3 getopt, for an example of the use of getopt(), and **follow the pattern in the example as much as possible**. Programming with getopt() is not for the faint of heart and requires a strong knowledge of both arrays and pointer in the C programming language. My most relevant experience with the parsing of command-line arguments was at NASA Goddard Space Flight Center working on ground control systems of spacecraft. Careful examination of multiple software systems comprising several million lines of C source code showed that, for the most critical of these systems, 44% of software errors came from processing arguments specified on a command line!

gets()

Syntax: int gets(char *) stdio library

gets function – reads an input string from standard input and places it in consecutive locations beginning in the one pointed to by the argument. Input is read until EOF or a newline character is read. The newline character is NOT placed into the array pointed to by the second argument. This treatment of the newline character is different from that of fgets().

USAGE: gets(char_ptr);

isalnum()

Syntax: int isalnum(char) std library

isalnum function – returns a nonzero value if the character is in one of the ranges A – Z , a – z, or 0 – 9; returns 0 otherwise – needs the include file ctype.h.

USAGE: if (isalnum(char_arg)) ...

isalpha()

Syntax: int isalpha(char) std library

isalpha function - returns a nonzero value if the character is in the range A – Z or a – z; returns 0 otherwise – needs the include file ctype.h.

USAGE: if (isalpha(char_arg))...

isdigit()

Syntax: int isdigit(char) std library

isdigit function – returns a nonzero value if the character is in the range 0 – 9; returns 0 otherwise – needs the include file ctype.h.

USAGE: if (isdigit(char_arg))...

islower()

Syntax: int islower(char) std library

islower function – returns a non-zero value if the character is in the range a – z; returns 0 otherwise – needs the include file ctype.h.

USAGE: if (islower(char_arg))...

isspace()

Syntax: int isspace(char) std library

isspace function: – returns a non-zero value if the argument is one of: blank, space, carriage return, form feed, vertical tab, newline; returns 0 otherwise – needs the include file ctype.h.

USAGE: if (isspace(char_arg))...

isupper()

Syntax: int isupper(char) std library

isupper function – returns a non-zero value if the character is in the range A – Z; returns 0 otherwise – needs the include file ctype.h.

USAGE: if (islower(char_arg))...

itoa()

Syntax: char* itoa(int) non-standard

itoa function – changes int to ASCII string - not always found in C libraries - see sprintf().

USGAE: string_val = itoa(int);

log()

Syntax: double log(double) math library

natural logarithm function

USAGE: double_result = log(double_argument)

log10()

Syntax: double log10(double) math library

logarithm to base 10 function

USAGE: double_result = log10(double_argument)

malloc()

Syntax: (void *) malloc(unsigned int) std library

NOTE: Many UNIX implementations have two versions of this function. One is in the standard library and the other is in the malloc library. To use the malloc library, include the file malloc.h and compile with the -lmalloc option.

malloc() returns a pointer to a region of size number of bytes; pointer is to char in Kernighan and Ritchie C and pointer is to void in ANSI C. The int parameter should always be positive.

USAGE: pointer = malloc(size)

memcpy()

Syntax: (char *) memcpy(char *, char*, unsigned int) string.h

function memcpy – behaves much like the function strcpy() - copies from the memory location pointed to by the second argument to the location pointed to by the first argument.; the number of characters copied is given by the third argument. The value returned is a pointer indicating the location of the second argument.

USAGE: source_ptr = memcpy(dest_ptr, source_ptr, num_bytes);

pow()

Syntax: double pow(double,double) math library

power function – raises the first argument to the second argument

USAGE: double_result = pow(double_arg1, double_arg2)

printf()

Syntax: int printf(char *, var_args) stdio library

printf function – prints to standard output according to the control specifications in the first argument. The variables that get their values printed are in the remaining arguments. See also the function scanf().

USAGE: printf(control_char_string, other args);

putc()

Syntax: int putc(char, FILE *) stdio.h

putc function – places the character argument on the output file pointed to by the file pointer specified in the second argument, which is a pointer to a FILE. The return value is the int equivalent of the first argument. See also fputc(), which has equivalent action.

USAGE: int_val = putc(ch, file_ptr);

putchar()

Syntax: int putchar(char) stdio.h

putchar function – writes its argument to the output stream stdout. The return value is the int equivalent of the argument.

USAGE: int_val = putchar(ch);

puts()

Syntax: int puts(char *) stdio.h

puts function – takes its argument, which is a character string, and places it on the output stream stdout. The first argument must be terminated by a null byte; this null byte is not written to the output stream.

There is one difference between puts() and fputs(). The function puts() always places a newline character at the end of the character stream, while fputs() does not. See also fputs().

USAGE: int_val = puts(char_ptr);

scanf()

Syntax: int scanf(char *, var_args) stdio library

scanf function – reads from standard input according to the control specifications in the first argument. The variables that get assigned values are in the remaining arguments.

USAGE: scanf(control_char_string, other args);

sin()

Syntax: double sin(double) math library

sine function

USAGE: double_result = sin(double_argument)

sinh()

Syntax: double sinh(double) math library

hyperbolic sine function

USAGE: double_result = sinh(double_argument)

sprintf()

Syntax: int sprintf(char *, char *, var_args) stdio library

sprintf function – prints its output to the string specified in the first argument according to the control specifications in the second argument. The variables that get their values printed are in the remaining arguments. See also the functions printf() and scanf().

USAGE: sprintf(result_string, control_char_string, other args);

sqrt()

Syntax: double sqrt(double) math library

square root function – error if argument is negative

USAGE: double_result = sqrt(double_argument).

sscanf()

Syntax: int sscanf(char *, char *, var_args) stdio library

sscanf function -– reads from character string specified in the first argument according to the control specifications in the second argument. The variables that get assigned values are in the remaining arguments.

USAGE: fscanf(file_ptr, control_char_string, other args);

strcat()

Syntax: (char *) strcat(char *, char *) string.h

strcat function concatenates the contents of the string pointed to by the second argument onto the end of the string pointed to by the first argument. The value of the first argument is returned. (The end-of-string character of the string pointed to by the first argument is overwritten by the characters from the string pointed to by the second argument.)

USAGE: string_ptr = strcat(string_ptr1, string_ptr2);

strcmp()

Syntax: int strcmp(char *, char *) string.h

strcmp function compares the contents of the string pointed to by the second argument with the string pointed to by the first argument. The function returns a negative value if the first string is lexicographically less than the second, a positive value if the first is greater than the second, and 0 if the strings are identical. Since lexicographical order is what is used in dictionaries, this function is useful for sorting alphabetic data.

USAGE: int_value = strcmp(string_ptr1, string_ptr2);

strcpy()

Syntax: (char *) strcpy(char *, char *)
string.h

strcpy function copies the contents of the string pointed to by the second argument into the string pointed to by the first argument at the beginning of that string. The value of the first argument is returned. (The end of string character from the string pointed to by the second argument is used to terminate the string.)

USAGE: string_ptr = strcpy(string_ptr1, string_ptr2);

strlen()

Syntax: int strlen(char *)
string.h

strlen function gives the length of the string pointed to by the second argument as an int; all characters up to, but not including, the end-of-string marker, are counted. The value of this int is nonnegative since the length of an empty string is 0.

USAGE: string_length = strlen(string_ptr);

tan()

Syntax: double tan(double) math library

tangent function

USAGE: double_result = tan(double_argument)

ungetc()

Syntax: int ungetc(char, char *) stdio library

ungetc function – places the character back on the specified input stream to be read by the next call to a "get" function such as getc(), getchar(), fgetc(), fgetchar(), etc.

USAGE: int_val = ungetc(ch, file_name);

References

Bach, M. J., *The Design of The UNIX Operating System*, Prentice-Hall, Englewood Cliffs, New Jersey, 1986.

Bourne, S. R., "UNIX Time-Sharing System: The UNIX Shell," *Bell Sys. Tech. J.*, vol. 57, no. 6, pp. 1971-1990, 1978.

Bovet, D. P, and M. Cesati, *Processes, Lightweight Processes, and Threads:. Understanding the Linux Kernel*, 3rd ed., O'Reilly Media, 2005.

Johnson, S. C. and D. M. Ritchie, "UNIX Time-Sharing System: Portability of C Programs and the UNIX System," *Bell Sys. Tech. J.*, vol. 57, no. 6, pp. 2021-2048, 1978.

Kernighan, B. W. and R. Pike, *Advanced Programming in the UNIX Environment*, Prentice-Hall, Englewood Cliffs, New Jersey, 1984.

Kernighan, B. W., and D. M. Ritchie, *The C Programming Language, second edition*, Prentice Hall, Englewood Cliffs, New Jersey, 1988.

Kernighan, B. W., and R. Pike, *The UNIX Programming Environment*, Prentice-Hall, Englewood Cliffs, New Jersey, 1984.

Leach, R. J., *Advanced Topics in UNIX*, John Wiley, New York, 1993.

Leach, R. J., *Advanced Topics in UNIX, second edition*, 2012.

Leach, R. J., *Using C in Software Design, second edition*, 2012.

Leffler, S., McCusick, M. K., Karels, M. J., and J. S. Quarterman, *The Design of the BSD UNIX Operating System*, Addison-Wesley, Reading, MA, 1989.

Raymond, Eric S., *The Art of UNIX Programming, Addison-Wesley Professional*, Reading, Massachusetts, 2003.

Ritchie, D. M., "UNIX Time-Sharing System: A Retrospective," *Bell Sys. Tech. J.*, vol. 57, no. 6, pp. 1947-1969, 1978. Also in Proc. Hawaii International Conference on Systems Science, Honolulu, Hawaii, Jan. 1977.

Ritchie, D. M., S. C. Johnson, M. E. Lesk, and B. W. Kernighan, "UNIX Time-Sharing System: The C Programming Language," *Bell Sys. Tech. J.*, vol. 57, no. 6, pp. 1991-2019, 1978.

Robbins, K. A., and S. Robbins, *Practical UNIX Programming: A Guide to Concurrency, Communications, and Multithreading*, Prentice-Hall, Englewood Cliffs, New Jersey, 1996.

Rochkind, Marc J., *Advanced UNIX Programming*, Prentice-Hall, Englewood Cliffs, New Jersey, 1985.

Rochkind, Marc J., *Advanced UNIX Programming, second edition*, Addison Wesley Professional, Reading, Massachusetts, 2004.

Sobell, Mark G., *A Practical Guide to Linux Commands, Editors, and Shell Programming (3rd Edition)* Prentice-Hall, Upper Saddle River, New Jersey, 2010.

Sobell, Mark G., *A Practical Guide to Fedora and Red Hat Enterprise Linux, Sixth Edition,* Prentice-Hall, Upper Saddle River, New Jersey, 2012.

Sobell, Mark G., *A Practical Guide to Ubuntu Linux (3rd Edition)* Prentice-Hall, Upper Saddle River, New Jersey, 2010.

Southerton, A., *Modern UNIX*, John Wiley & Sons, New York, New York, 1992.

Stevens, W. R., *Advanced Programming in the UNIX Environment*, Addison-Wesley, Reading, Massachusetts, 1992.

Stevens, W. R., and Stephen A. Rago, *Advanced Programming in the UNIX Environment, second edition*, Addison-Wesley Professional, Reading, Massachusetts, 2005.

Stevens, W. R., *UNIX Network Programming*, Prentice-Hall, Englewood Cliffs, New Jersey, 1991.

Index

Cover design by Ronald J. Leach, AfterMath

Book design by Ronald J. Leach

Printed in the United States of America

First Printing: November 2012

CPSIA information can be obtained at www.ICGtesting.com
Printed in the USA
BVOW04s2215090914

366188BV00008B/91/P

9 781939 142306